Focus: Grades 3-5 Economics

Barbara J. Flowers
Penny Kugler
Bonnie T. Meszaros
Layna Stiles
Mary C. Suiter

National Council on Economic Education

Authors

Barbara J. Flowers
Associate Director
Center for Entrepreneurship
and Economic Education
University of Missouri-St. Louis

Penny Kugler
Director
Center for Economic Education
Central Missouri State University

Bonnie T. Meszaros
Associate Director
Center for Economic Education
and Entrepreneurship
University of Delaware

Layna Stiles
Fourth-grade teacher
Holly Hill Elementary
West Clermont School District
Amelia, Ohio

Mary C. Suiter
Director
Center for Entrepreneurship
and Economic Education
University of Missouri-St. Louis

PROJECT DIRECTOR:
Mary C. Suiter
Director
Center for Entrepreneurship
and Economic Education
University of Missouri-St. Louis

PROJECT EDITOR:
Lawrence State

DESIGN:
Susan Todd

FUNDING

The **National Council on Economic Education** gratefully acknowledges the funding of this publication by the **U.S. Department of Education, Office of Safe and Drug-Free Schools** under PR Grant Q304B040002. Any opinions, findings, conclusions, or recommendations expressed in this publication are those of the authors and do not necessarily reflect the view of the U.S. Department of Education.

ISBN 1-56183-535-8

Acknowledgments

ECONOMIC CONTENT REVIEW:
Curt L. Anderson
Director
Center for Economic Education
University of Minnesota - Duluth

REVIEWERS:
Mimi Baden
Solomon Schecter Day School
St. Louis, Missouri

Kelly Bolen
Greenbrier Elementary
Greenville County Schools
Greenville, South Carolina

Nancy L. Carter
Benjamin Banneker Elementary School
Milford School District
Milford, Delaware

Tatiana Chorna
School #46
Kharkov, Ukraine

Charles S. Collier
Harmony Elementary School
Mount Baker School District
Bellingham, Washington

Erin Donohoo
Holly Hill Elementary
West Clermont School District
Amelia, Ohio

Rebecca King
Montgomery Intermediate School
Montgomery Independent School District
Montgomery, Texas

Marilyn Johnson
Holly Hill Elementary
West Clermont School District
Amelia, Ohio

Deborah A. Lawson
Sterling Elementary
Warrensburg, Missouri

Jeanine Moore
Long Neck Elementary
Indian River School District
Millsboro, Delaware

Irina Romaneyeva
Valentina Tomayeva Advanced
English Language and Economics
Study School #29
Kharkov, Ukraine

Janice Trainer
Etta J. Wilson School
Christina School District
Newark, Delaware

Vicki Weiss
City School
Grand Blanc School District
Grand Blanc, Michigan

Contents

Foreword

Focus: Grades 3-5 Economics is a core publication of the National Council on Economic Education (NCEE). NCEE believes that students can begin learning economics early and that important progress can be made in grades 3-5. The Focus series demonstrates how economics can enhance learning in a variety of subjects and at all grade levels. Activities in this publication are interactive, reflecting the belief that students learn best through active, highly personalized experiences with economics. Application of economic understanding to real-world situations and contexts dominate the lessons. In addition, the lessons explicitly teach the Voluntary National Content Standards in Economics, specifically the benchmarks for grades 3-5.

The development of this publication was undertaken as part of the Cooperative Civic Education and Economic Education Exchange Program (CEEP) funded by the United States Department of Education under PR Grant Q304B040002. NCEE extends deep appreciation to the U.S. Department of Education for its support of this program. We thank our program officer, Ms. Rita Foy Moss, Office of Safe and Drug-Free Schools, U.S. Department of Education. We are grateful that the U.S. Congress had the foresight to realize the need for economic education in emerging and developing market economies and the vision to see how an international exchange program such as the CEEP could benefit U.S. teachers and students.

The NCEE thanks the authors, drawn from NCEE's talented network of affiliated Councils and Centers, particularly project leader Mary Suiter, director of the Center for Entrepreneurship and Economic Education at the University of Missouri-St. Louis, and authors Barbara Flowers, associate director of the Center for Entrepreneurship and Economic Education at the University of Missouri-St. Louis; Penny Kugler, director of the Center for Economic Education at Central Missouri State University; Bonnie Meszaros, associate director of the Center for Economic Education and Entrepreneurship at the University of Delaware; and Layna Stiles, fourth-grade teacher at Holly Hill Elementary, West Clermont School District, Ohio.

Robert F. Duvall, Ph.D.
President and CEO
National Council on Economic Education

Content Standards: **Economics**

Standard 1

- **Benchmark 3 for 4th grade:** Goods are objects that can satisfy people's wants.
- **Benchmark 4 for 4th grade:** Services are actions that can satisfy people's wants.
- **Benchmark 6 for 4th grade:** Whenever a choice is made, something is given up.
- **Benchmark 7 for 4th grade:** The opportunity cost of a choice is the value of the best alternative given up.
- **Benchmark 8 for 4th grade:** People whose wants are satisfied by using goods and services are called consumers.
- **Benchmark 9 for 4th grade:** Productive resources are the natural resources, human resources and capital goods available to make goods and services.
- **Benchmark 10 for 4th grade:** Natural resources, such as land, are "gifts of nature"; they are present without human intervention.
- **Benchmark 11 for 4th grade:** Human resources are the quantity and quality of human effort directed toward producing goods and services.
- **Benchmark 12 for 4th grade:** Capital goods (resources) are goods produced and used to make other goods and services.
- **Benchmark 15 for 4th grade:** People who make goods and provide services are called producers.
- **Benchmark 1 for 8th grade:** Scarcity is the condition of not being able to have all of the goods and services that one wants. It exists because human wants for goods and services exceed the quantity of goods and services that can be produced using all available resources.

Standard 5

- **Benchmark 6 for 8th Grade:** Voluntary exchange among people or organizations in different countries gives people a broader range of choices in buying goods and services.

Standard 6

- **Benchmark 1 for 4th grade:** Economic specialization occurs when people concentrate their production on fewer kinds of goods and services than they consume.
- **Benchmark 2 for 4th grade:** Division of labor occurs when the production of a good is broken down into numerous separate tasks, with different workers performing each task.
- **Benchmark 3 for 4th grade:** Specialization and division of labor usually increase the productivity of workers.
- **Benchmark 4 for 4th grade:** Greater specialization leads to increased interdependence among producers and consumers.

Standard 7

- **Benchmark 1 for 4th grade:** A price is what people pay when they buy a good or service and what they receive when they sell a good or service.
- **Benchmark 2 for 4th grade:** A market exists whenever buyers and sellers exchange goods and services.
- **Benchmark 3 for 4th grade:** Most people both produce and consume. As producers they make goods and services; as consumers they use goods and services.

Content Standards: (continued) **Economics**

Standard 8

- **Benchmark 1 for 4th grade:** Higher prices for a good or service provide incentives for buyers to purchase less of that good or service and for producers to make or sell more of it. Lower prices for a good or service provide incentives for buyers to purchase more of that good or service and for producers to make or sell less of it.

- **Benchmark 1 for 8th grade:** An increase in the price of a good or service encourages people to look for substitutes, causing the quantity demanded to decrease, and vice versa. This relationship between price and quantity demanded, known as the law of demand, exists as long as other factors influencing demand do not change.

Standard 9

- **Benchmark 2 for 4th grade:** Competition among sellers results in lower costs and prices, higher product quality and better customer service.
- **Benchmark 1 for 8th grade:** Sellers compete on the basis of price, product quality, customer service, product design and variety, and advertising.

Standard 10

- **Benchmark 1 for 4th grade:** Banks are institutions where people save money and earn interest, and where other people borrow money and pay interest.
- **Benchmark 2 for 4th grade:** Saving is the part of income not spent on taxes or consumption.
- **Benchmark 1 for 8th grade:** Banks and other financial institutions channel funds from savers to borrowers and investors.

Standard 11

- **Benchmark 1 for 4th grade:** Money is anything widely accepted as final payment for goods and services.
- **Benchmark 3 for 4th grade:** People consume goods and services, not money; money is useful primarily because it can be used to buy goods and services.
- **Benchmark 4 for 4th grade:** Producers use natural resources, human resources and capital goods (not money) to make goods and services.

Standard 13

- **Benchmark 1 for 4th grade:** Labor is a human resource used to produce goods and services.
- **Benchmark 2 for 4th grade:** People can earn income by exchanging their human resources (physical or mental work) for wages or salaries.
- **Benchmark 1 for 8th grade:** Employers are willing to pay wages and salaries to workers because they expect to sell the goods and services those workers produce at prices high enough to cover the wages and salaries and all other costs of production.
- **Benchmark 2 for 8th grade:** To earn income, people sell productive resources. These include their labor, capital, natural resources, and entrepreneurial talents.

Content Standards: (continued) **Economics**

Standard 14

- **Benchmark 1 for 4th grade:** Entrepreneurs are individuals who are willing to take risks to develop new products and start new businesses. They recognize opportunities, enjoy working for themselves, and accept challenges.
- **Benchmark 2 for 4th grade:** An invention is a new product. Innovation is the introduction of an invention into a use that has economic value.
- **Benchmark 3 for 4th grade:** Entrepreneurs often are innovative. They attempt to solve problems by developing and marketing new or improved products.
- **Benchmark 3 for 8th grade:** Entrepreneurs and other sellers earn profits when buyers purchase the products they sell at prices high enough to cover the costs of production.
- **Benchmark 4 for 8th grade:** Entrepreneurs and other sellers incur losses when buyers do not purchase the products they sell at prices high enough to cover the costs of production.

Standard 16

- **Benchmark 1 for 4th grade:** Governments provide certain kinds of goods and services in a market economy.
- **Benchmark 2 for 4th grade:** Governments pay for the goods and services they use or provide by taxing or borrowing from the people.

A Correlation of the Lessons with the Voluntary National Content Standards in Economics

		Lessons	1	2	3	4	5	6	7	8	9	10	11	12	13	14
Standard	**Benchmark**															
Standard 1	3 for 4th grade	Goods												•		
	4 for 4th grade	Services												•		
	6 for 4th grade	Choices require giving something up		•												
	7 for 4th grade	Opportunity cost		•												
	8 for 4th grade	Consumers												•		
	9 for 4th grade	Productive resources	•													
	10 for 4th grade	Natural resources	•	•			•									
	11 for 4th grade	Human resources	•	•			•									
	12 for 4th grade	Capital goods (resources)	•				•									
	15 for 4th grade	Producers												•		
	1 for 8th grade	Scarcity		•												
Standard 5	1 for 8th grade	Why people trade														•
Standard 6	1 for 4th grade	Specialization							•							•
	2 for 4th grade	Division of labor							•							
	3 for 4th grade	Specialization and division of labor							•							
	4 for 4th grade	Specialization and interdependence														•
Standard 7	1 for 4th grade	Price											•			
	2 for 4th grade	Market													•	
	3 for 4th grade	Producers and consumers													•	
Standard 8	1 for 4th grade	Prices provide incentives to buyers											•			
	1 for 8th grade	Law of demand											•			
Standard 9	2 for 4th grade	Competition among sellers								•						
	1 for 8th grade	How sellers compete								•						
Standard 10	1 for 4th grade	Banks									•					
	2 for 4th grade	Saving									•					
	1 for 8th grade	Banks channel funds									•					
Standard 11	1 for 4th grade	What is money										•				
	3 for 4th grade	Money is useful for consumers													•	
	4 for 4th grade	Money is useful for producers													•	
Standard 13	1 for 4th grade	Labor													•	
	2 for 4th grade	Income				•									•	
	1 for 8th grade	Why employers pay for resources													•	
	2 for 8th grade	How people earn income													•	
Standard 14	1 for 4th grade	What is an entrepreneur						•								
	2 for 4th grade	Invention and innovation						•								
	3 for 4th grade	Entrepreneurs are innovative						•								
	3 for 8th grade	How entrepreneurs earn profit					•	•								
	4 for 8th grade	How entrepreneurs incur loss					•									
Standard 16	1 for 4th grade	Governments provide goods			•	•										
	2 for 4th grade	How governments pay for goods			•	•										

International Connections

These suggestions are provided for teachers in countries other than the United States who might use these lessons.

These suggestions are also provided for United States teachers who may wish to include a more international perspective for their students. These suggestions might be beneficial if your class includes immigrants from other countries, if you are studying different regions of the world, or if you are asking students to study their cultural heritage.

Lesson 1: Rolling for Resources
The students learn about three categories of productive resources. Adapt the list of resources used in the lesson to include resources that are important to a particular country and have the students identify the country with which these resources are associated. For example, the list might include: oil, diamonds, coal, computers, fishing boats, sewing machines, rice farmers and shoe makers.

Lesson 2: Back-to-School Scarcity
The students experience scarcity when they produce decorations representing goods related to going to school – scissors, globe, pencil and school bus. Adapt the lesson by using a variety of decorations, depending on the theme or topic being taught, the season or the month of the year. These goods might represent holiday decorations, national monuments and symbols, or imported or exported goods from a particular country.

Lesson 3: We've Got Goods
The students learn about privately produced and government-provided goods in the United States. The mix of private goods and those provided by government varies from country to country. Adapt this list using examples of both types of goods from a particular country.

Lesson 4: A Taxing Situation
The students learn about taxes that U.S. citizens usually pay – income tax, property tax and sales tax. They learn the formula for calculating the tax: r X B = T. Adapt the lesson by identifying the types of taxes paid in another country and incorporating the appropriate formula and situations. Or, compare taxes paid in the United States to the types of taxes paid in another country.

Lesson 5: Flagging Profits
The students produce flags to learn about profit and loss. The lesson uses a generic flag appropriate for a national holiday. Adapt the lesson by using flags from different countries. Instead of flags, students might produce an item that represents an important holiday in another country.

Lesson 6: My Problem, My Solution
The students consider the problems that would lead a person to develop specific products. The students learn the meanings of opportunity recognition, invention, entrepreneurs and innovation.

Choose a country based on climate or geological features. For example, Niger is mostly desert; it is very dry and dusty. The students could brainstorm types of products that might be developed to help grow crops, to protect people's skin, or to keep people cool. For example, an entrepreneur could develop a large hat, the size of an umbrella, that would allow a person to stay shaded even when in an area with no protection from the sun.

International Connections (continued)

Lesson 7: The Shape of Production

The students produce various shapes – square, rhombus, triangle, rectangle – to learn about productivity, specialization of labor and specialization of production. This lesson can be used as written to teach students in other countries that specialization of labor and specialization of production lead to increased productivity.

Lesson 8: Competing for Buyers

The students learn that sellers compete for customers based on price, product quality, customer service, product design and variety, and advertising. Have the students investigate whether students in another country would be interested in similar products, and whether producers in that country provide similar types of customer service.

Adapt the lessons for use in another country by incorporating products with which students in that country would be familiar. This will necessarily change the examples regarding customer service, product design and variety, and advertising.

Lesson 9: Bulletin-Board Banking

The students learn that banks are businesses in the community that accept deposits and make loans. They also learn that interest is the price paid for using someone else's money.

In some countries, people do not think banks are safe places in which to keep their money. Discuss how mistrust of banks might affect a country's economy. The discussion could focus on the following points:

- If people do not think they can get their money from the bank when they want to, they would not be willing to put their money in the bank.
- If people do not keep their money in banks, where might they keep it?
- If people do not keep their money in banks, banks would not have as much money to lend.
- If banks are unable to make loans, people would have to postpone large purchases.

Lesson 10: What Makes Money Acceptable?

The students learn about the characteristics of money – portable, durable, divisible, acceptable and relatively scarce. They also learn about the security features found on U.S. currency and why security features are important for protecting the integrity of a country's currency. Substitute another country's currency and discuss its security features. Compare U.S. currency with another country's currency.

Lesson 11: How Many Snacks Will the Students Buy?

The students learn about the law of demand by investigating how many snacks students in the classroom are willing and able to buy at various prices. This lesson can be adapted for use in another country by substituting snacks students in that country are likely to consume and by using prices expressed in that country's currency.

International Connections (continued)

Lesson 12: Neighborhood Producers and Consumers
The students learn that people are both producers and consumers. Adapt the lesson by explaining that some goods we consume come from producers in other countries, and that the country in which a good is made is usually identified somewhere on the good. Have the students participate in a scavenger hunt. The scavenger hunt can take place at school or be assigned as homework. Provide a list to students similar to the following:

Made in China ______________________________

Made in France ______________________________

Made in Sri Lanka ____________________________

When the students have completed the scavenger hunt, pose questions regarding the goods produced in other countries, where the country is on a world map, how the good gets to the students' country, and who in their country consumes the good.

Lesson 13: Moving in Economic Circles
The students learn about the simple circular flow of a market economy. Adapt this lesson by explaining that even though a business is located in the students' country, it could be owned by people in another country. The students can ask working adults whether the company for which they work is owned domestically or is a company with foreign ownership. Some examples of foreign-owned companies producing goods and services in the United States are Unilever, Saint Gobain, ABB and Toyota Motor Corporation.

Domestically-owned businesses might have plants operating in other countries. The students can ask working adults whether the company for which they work has plants in other countries. Some examples of American-owned companies operating plants in other countries are Hussman Corporation, Ford Motor Corporation, General Motors Corporation and Anheuser-Busch.

Lesson 14: Tic-Tac-Toe Trade
The students act as citizens in two different countries. They produce "X's" and "O's" for tic-tac-toe. They discover what happens if one country specializes in the production of "X's" and the other specializes in the production of "O's." This lesson can be taught as-is to highlight the reason for and benefits of trade.

Follow this lesson with a research project. Each student in a class could select a country and conduct research to determine the country's imports, exports and trade partners.

Lesson 1 - **Rolling for Resources**

LESSON DESCRIPTION

This lesson is designed to introduce the concept of productive resources and to have the students identify productive resources as human resources, natural resources or capital resources (goods). By playing a game, the students practice identifying and categorizing various resources. The game allows the students to assess their knowledge of resources and can also be used as an enrichment-station activity.

CONCEPTS

Capital resources (goods)
Human resources
Natural resources
Productive resources

CONTENT STANDARD

Standard 1 – Scarcity

- **Benchmark 9 for 4th grade:** Productive resources are the natural resources, human resources and capital goods available to make goods and services.
- **Benchmark 10 for 4th grade:** Natural resources, such as land, are "gifts of nature"; they are present without human intervention.
- **Benchmark 11 for 4th grade:** Human resources are the quantity and quality of human effort directed toward producing goods and services.
- **Benchmark 12 for 4th grade:** Capital goods (resources) are goods produced and used to make other goods and services.

OBJECTIVES

The students will:

1. Identify productive resources.
2. Define and give examples of natural, human and capital resources.
3. Distinguish among natural, human and capital resources.

TIME REQUIRED

45-60 minutes

MATERIALS

✄ Scissors
✓ Scotch tape
✓ Visuals 1.1 and 1.2
✓ One copy of Activities 1.1 and 1.2 for each group, printed on card stock and cut apart
✓ For each group of students, prepare one "game set" (a set of resource cards and one die):
✄ Cut out a die for each group, fold it into a cube and use tape to secure it.
✄ Cut out the resource cards. On the back of each human resource card, draw one small dot. On the back of each natural resource card, draw two small dots. On the back of each capital resource card, draw three small dots. By matching the number of dots on the die, students will be able to see if they have selected the correct resource card.
✓ One copy of Activities 1.3 and 1.4 for each student

PROCEDURE

1. Ask the students what things are necessary to produce or build a house. ***Answers will vary but should include such things as lumber, nails, saws, carpenters, drywall, roofers, and so on.*** Tell the students that **productive resources** are the things used to produce a good or service. Point out that productive resources can be placed into three groups – human resources, natural resources or capital resources.
2. Display Visual 1.1. Define the types of re-

sources as follows:

• **Human resources** are people who work to produce a good or service. Examples of human resources are a truck driver, plumber, teacher and nurse. Ask the students for other examples of human resources. Write the students' responses on the board.

• **Natural resources** are things that occur naturally in the world and can be used to produce a good or service. These resources are gifts of nature and are present without human intervention. Examples of natural resources are natural gas, granite, deer and minerals. Ask the students for other examples of natural resources. Write the students' responses on the board.

• **Capital resources** are goods produced and used to make other goods and services. Examples of capital resources are an office building, office copying machine, pots and pans and a wrench. Ask the students for other examples of capital resources. Write the students' responses on the board.

(**NOTE:** A hammer is a capital resource. Nails are intermediate goods. Both capital resources and intermediate goods are goods that are produced in order to produce other goods. Producing both capital resources and intermediate goods requires human, capital and natural resources. The difference between capital resources and intermediate goods is the role they play in producing those other goods. Capital resources provide productive services; they are the actors in the process–the tools. Intermediate goods provide the materials with which the goods are produced; they are acted upon–they are the stuff from which the goods are made.)

3. Explain to the students that human, natural and capital resources are all examples of productive resources used to make goods and services that people buy every day. Ask the students what things are necessary to produce a haircut. ***Answers will vary but should include such things as comb, razor, clippers, electricity, scissors, hair stylist, and so on.*** Ask the students to classify the productive resources used to produce a haircut as natural, human or capital resources. Record their answers on the board. ***Capital – comb, razor, clipper; natural – water; human – hair stylist***

4. Tell the students that they are going to play a game in small groups. Divide the class into groups of four or five students each. Distribute an already cut-apart copy of Activity 1.1 and an already-assembled copy of Activity 1.2 to each group.

5. Display Visual 1.2. Review the rules of the game as displayed on Visual 1.2.

6. Help the students determine who the youngest player is in their groups. Make certain that cards are dispersed so that all of the students in the group can see the resources. Allow time for the students to play.

7. When the groups have finished playing, distribute a copy of Activity 1.3 to each student. Instruct the students to identify the resource cards they selected during the game by writing the resource name in the correct space on Activity 1.3.

8. Once the students have identified the resource cards they collected, ask each student to think of a good or service that each resource could be used to produce. In the box next to each type of resource on Activity 1.3, instruct the students to either write a sentence containing the name of this good or service or draw a picture of the good or service.

9. Display the students' pictures and sentences on a bulletin board in the classroom for further discussion.

CLOSURE

10. Ask the following questions to review the main points of the lesson:

A. Why do people use productive resources? *To produce goods and services*

B. Name one of the three kinds of productive resources. ***Human, natural or capital resources***

C. What are natural resources? ***Things that occur in the world naturally and can be used to produce a good or service***

D. Give some examples of a natural resource. ***Water, soil, trees, cows, coal, sunlight***

E. What are human resources? ***People who do the work to provide a good or service***

F. Give some examples of human resources. ***Teacher, mechanic, nurse, carpenter, plumber, farmer***

G. What are capital resources? ***Things made by people and used to produce goods and services, such as tools, equipment, factories and machinery***

H. Give some examples of capital resources. ***Machines, office buildings, delivery trucks, computers, software, robots***

I. What are some human resources needed to build a house? ***Carpenter, electrician, architect***

J. What are some natural resources used to build a house? ***Land, stone, trees, sand***

K. What are some capital resources used to build a house? ***Hammer, saw, sawhorses, paint brush***

ASSESSMENT

Distribute a copy of Activity 1.4 to each student. Explain that in each picture there is a human resource, a natural resource and a capital resource. Tell the students they should identify a natural resource, a human resource and a capital resource in each picture and write the name of that resource in the appropriate space on the page.

Activity 3 answers:

Picture #1:
The human resource is ***a farmer.***
The natural resource is ***soil.***
The capital resource is ***a tractor.***

Picture #2:
The human resource is ***a florist.***
The natural resources are ***flowers.***
The capital resources are ***vases.***

Picture #3:
The human resource is ***a logger, chain saw operator.***
The natural resource is ***a tree.***
The capital resource is ***a chain saw.***

Visual 1.1 - **Rolling for Resources**

• HUMAN RESOURCES

• NATURAL RESOURCES

• CAPITAL RESOURCES

Visual 1.2 - **Rules for Rolling for Resources**

- ✓ Each group displays all of its resource cards face-up.

- ✓ Make certain the cards are scattered slightly so that each resource card is visible.

- ✓ To "win" the game, a student must collect a human resource card, a natural resource card and a capital resource card.

- ✓ The resource cards have dots on the back that match the dots for each type of resource on the die (human resources-one dot; natural resources-two dots; capital resources-three dots).

- ✓ The students will take turns rolling the die. Begin with the youngest student in the group. After that, play will move to the left.

Visual 1.2 - (continued)

Rules for Rolling for Resources

✓ If the die lands on "natural resource," the student should find a natural resource card from the deck of cards.

✓ If the die lands on "human resource," the student should find a human resource card from the deck of cards.

✓ If the die lands on "capital resource," the student should find a capital resource card from the deck of cards.

✓ If a student selects the correct resource card, the number on the back of the card will match the number of dots for the type of resource on the die.

✓ If a student selects a correct resource card from the deck of cards, he or she may keep the card, and his or her turn is over.

Visual 1.2 - (continued)

Rules for Rolling for Resources

- ✓ If the card selected isn't a correct example of the resource displayed on the die, the student must put the card back in the pile and wait for his or her next turn.

- ✓ If a student rolls the die and it lands on a resource for which he or she already has a card, he or she may roll a second time. If the die again lands on a type of resource for which he or she already has a card, he or she must wait until his or her next turn.

- ✓ The game is played until each student in the group has correctly selected cards for each type of resource.

Activity 1.1 - **Resource Cards**

DOCTOR	NURSE
TEACHER	PILOT
WAITRESS	FIREFIGHTER
CHEF	TAXI DRIVER
SECRETARY	ARTIST

(HUMAN RESOURCES ARE ON THIS PAGE)

Activity 1.1 - (continued) **Resource Cards**

STORE CLERK	ENGINEER
RODEO COWBOY	ACTOR
FLORIST	AUTHOR
CIRCUS CLOWN	BALLET DANCER
FARMER	LAWYER

(HUMAN RESOURCES ARE ON THIS PAGE)

Activity 1.1 - (continued) **Resource Cards**

SOIL	TREES
SUNLIGHT	SEEDS
STONE	COAL
AIR	CLAY
FISH	WIND

(NATURAL RESOURCES ARE ON THIS PAGE)

Activity 1.1 - (continued) **Resource Cards**

COPPER ORE	FEATHERS
HERBS	SAND
DIAMONDS	SUGAR CANE
OIL	WATER
GOLD ORE	IRON ORE

(NATURAL RESOURCES ARE ON THIS PAGE)

Activity 1.1 - (continued) **Resource Cards**

DESK	CHAIN SAW
HAMMER	COMPUTER
PLOW	CALCULATOR
FORK LIFT	SCISSORS
TRACTOR	PAINT BRUSH

(CAPITAL RESOURCES ARE ON THIS PAGE)

Activity 1.1 - (continued) **Resource Cards**

DUMP TRUCK	TELEPHONE
SHOVEL	BULLDOZER
FIRE HOSE	MICROSCOPE
FISHING POLE	CASH REGISTER
VACUUM CLEANER	SEWING MACHINE

(CAPITAL RESOURCES ARE ON THIS PAGE)

Activity 1.2 - **Die Cut-Out**

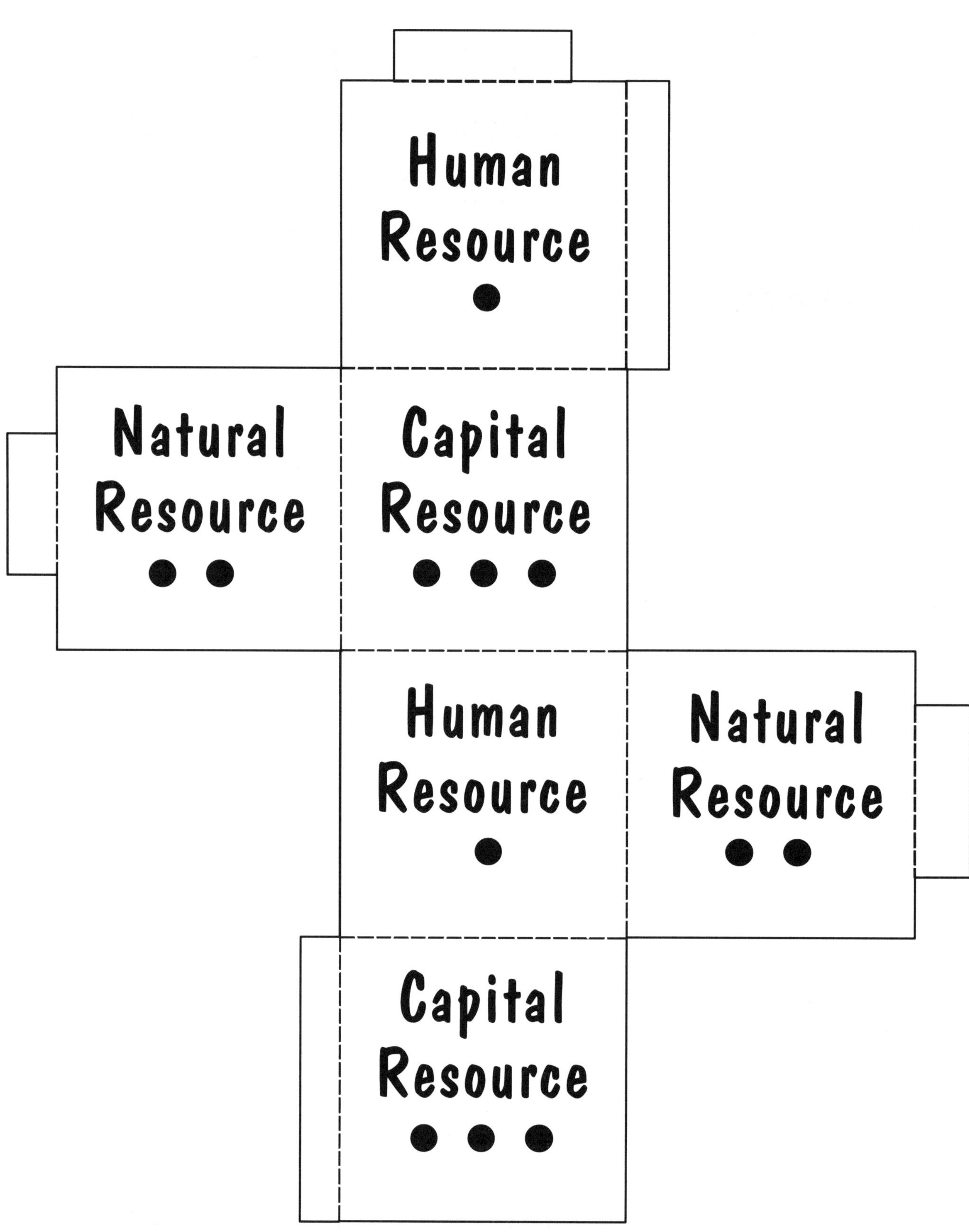

Activity 1.3 - **Resource Worksheet**

	A GOOD OR SERVICE THAT THIS RESOURCE CAN PRODUCE IS....
The HUMAN RESOURCE on my card was ______________.	
The NATURAL RESOURCE on my card was ______________.	
The CAPITAL RESOURCE on my card was ______________.	

Activity 1.4 - **Assessment**

Identify the types of resources in each picture below.

	1. The human resource is ______________________. 2. The natural resource is ______________________. 3. The capital resource is ______________________.
	1. The human resource is ______________________. 2. The natural resource is ______________________. 3. The capital resource is ______________________.
	1. The human resource is ______________________. 2. The natural resource is ______________________. 3. The capital resource is ______________________.

 FOCUS: GRADES 3 – 5 ECONOMICS,

Lesson 2 - **Back-to-School Scarcity**

LESSON DESCRIPTION

While producing classroom decorations, student groups realize there is a scarcity of human resources. There are not enough students to produce the quantity of decorations the teacher requests in the time allowed. Because of scarcity each group must select one of the four decorations to produce. Groups use a decision-making grid to help them decide what to produce and then identify the opportunity cost of their decision.

CONCEPTS

Human resources
Natural resources
Opportunity cost
Scarcity

CONTENT STANDARD

Standard 1 – Scarcity

- **Benchmark 6 for 4th grade:** Whenever a choice is made, something is given up.
- **Benchmark 7 for 4th grade:** The opportunity cost of a choice is the value of the best alternative given up.
- **Benchmark 10 for 4th grade:** Natural resources, such as land, are "gifts of nature"; they are present without human intervention.
- **Benchmark 11 for 4th grade:** Human resources are the quantity and quality of human effort directed toward producing goods and services.
- **Benchmark 1 for 8th grade:** Scarcity is the condition of not being able to have all of the goods and services that one wants. It exists because human wants for goods and services exceed the quantity of goods and services that can be produced using all available resources.

OBJECTIVES

The students will:

1. Define human resources, natural resources, scarcity and opportunity cost.
2. Give examples of scarcity situations.
3. Identify the opportunity cost when making a decision.
4. Explain why scarcity necessitates making choices.
5. Explain how scarcity of resources affects what can be produced.

TIME REQUIRED

60 minutes

MATERIALS

✓ Visuals 2.1 and 2.2
✓ (Optional) Visual 2.3
✓ One copy of Activity 2.1 on poster board for each group
✓ One copy of Activities 2.2 and 2.4 for each student
✓ (Optional) One copy of Activity 2.3 for each student
✓ Prior to start of lesson, make one copy of Activity 2.1 and cut out patterns
✓ Yellow, tan, black, and green paper:
  Five sheets of each per group in Round 1;
  Enough of each color for groups to produce 10 of each decoration in Round 2
✂ One pair of scissors
✓ One pencil per student
✓ One large sheet of paper and one marker for each group
✓ Masking tape

PROCEDURE

1. Write "Back-to-School" on the board. Ask the students what visuals or words come to mind when they think of getting ready to go back to school in the fall. ***Homework, school buses, crayons, pencils, notebook*** (**NOTE:** This lesson can be adapted for other themes.)

2. Tell the students that they are going to make some decorations for the classroom that reflect the theme, "Back-to-School."

3. Show the students the cutouts for a pencil, school bus, globe and pair of scissors from Activity 2.1.

4. Explain that the students will work in groups to produce 10 of each of these items.

5. Display Visual 2.1.

6. Review the specifications for producing the classroom decorations.

   ✂ Cut out the pattern for each decoration from Activity 2.1. (If a different theme is being used, prepare a page of patterns for the students.)

   • Make sure the pattern has smooth edges.

   • Trace the pattern on colored paper as follows:

   ✎ Yellow for the school bus
   ✎ Tan for the pencil
   ✎ Green for the scissors
   ✎ Black for the globe

   ✂ Cut out 10 of each product.

7. Divide the students into groups of three. Give each group three pencils, three pair of scissors and one copy of Activity 2.1. Allow time for the groups to cut out the patterns. Once all the groups have cut out the patterns, give each group five sheets each of green, black, yellow and tan paper.

8. Impress upon the students the importance of cutting out each decoration carefully and one at a time so that each completed product has smooth edges.

9. Inform the students they will have 15 minutes to produce their assigned items.

10. Stop production after 10 minutes. Ask the students to inspect their work to be sure that each cutout is of good quality. Inspect the products and collect all that are not produced to specifications.

11. Resume production.

12. Stop production after five minutes. Inspect final products. Collect all that are incomplete or poorly made. Collect all unused colored paper. Ask the groups to count the total of each type of decoration produced.

13. Discuss the following questions:

    A. How many groups had enough colored paper to produce 10 of each decoration? ***All***

    B. How many groups had enough scissors and pencils to produce 10 of each decoration? ***All***

    C. How many groups produced 10 of each decoration? ***None*** Why? ***Not enough workers. Some students may say not enough time. Point out that the time was set by the teacher and cannot change and that if there had been more workers in each group, more could have been produced in the same amount of time.***

14. Explain that the groups did not have enough human resources to complete the task. Explain that **human resources** are people who work to produce a good or service.

15. Ask the students how they were human resources in the production activity. ***They produced a good, the decorations.*** Ask for examples of other human resources at school. ***Teacher, bus driver, principal, crossing guard, custodian, cafeteria worker***

16. Tell the students that in the production activity, they experienced a problem of scarcity. **Scarcity** means not having enough resources to produce everything people want. Ask the students what was scarce in their production activity. ***Human resources***

17. Ask the students if there are times when they experience scarcity at school or at home. ***Answers will vary but might include games, playground equipment, time to watch television.*** Provide the following examples and ask the students to identify what is scarce in each situation.

    A. Twenty-six students have one hour in a computer lab which has only 10 computers. Each student wants one hour on a computer to complete an assignment. ***Computers are scarce.***

    B. There are only three copies of a favorite book in the school library. There are 12 students who want to check out the book. ***Books are scarce.***

    C. There are 48 lockers for the fifth-grade class. All 69 fifth-graders want their own locker. ***Lockers are scarce.***

18. Explain to the students that because of a scarcity of human resources, they could not produce all four products. Because all the students in the class were producing, there were no additional workers to add to the production of decorations. Because the class cannot produce all four of the decorations, it must make choices.

19. Display Visual 2.2. (**NOTE:** If another theme is being used, use Visual 2.3.) Tell the students that this is a decision-making grid that will help the groups decide which decorations to produce.

20. Ask the students to define the scarcity problem. ***There are not enough human resources to produce all four decorations.*** Write the students' correct response on Visual 2.2.

21. Point out that the four decorations they could produce are pictured under the heading "alternatives."

22. Explain that criteria are the things that are important to consider when making a decision. For this activity, some of the criteria will be: "easy to cut out," "represents back-to-school theme," "could be enhanced with pictures or drawings," and "interesting to look at." Point out that these are written in the first row of boxes on the decision-making grid. Ask the students if they can think of other important things to consider when making this decision. ***Answers will vary.*** Add relevant suggestions to the decision-making grid.

23. Tell the students that they will evaluate each alternative against the criteria by placing a "plus" in the box if the alternative meets a criterion and a "minus" if it does not. Demonstrate by asking the class the following:

    A. Was the pencil easy for members of the group to cut out? ***Answers will vary by group. In this all-class example, place a "plus/minus" in the box.*** Explain that when each group makes this decision, the group will place either a "plus" sign or a "minus" sign in the box.

    B. Does the pencil represent the theme? ***Yes*** Place a "plus" sign in the box.

    C. Would it be easy to paste pictures or draw pictures on the pencil? ***No*** Place a "minus" sign in the box.

    D. Is the pencil interesting to look at? ***No*** Place a "minus" sign in the box.

    E. What is the net value? *[+1 + (-2) = -1]* The students may need help in adding positive and negative numbers. (**NOTE:** For younger students, just count the number of "plus" signs.)

24. Distribute a copy of Activity 2.2 to each student. If another theme is being used, distribute Activity 2.3. Ask the students to work in their groups to complete the grid.

25. Distribute a large sheet of paper and a marker to each group. Tell the groups to copy their

completed decision-making grid onto their paper and place a star next to their decision.

26. Have the groups tape their grids on the board and share their decisions.

27. Ask the students why all the groups didn't make the same decision. ***Groups valued the criteria differently.***

28. Ask each group for its second choice. ***The alternative with the second-highest net value, or, for younger students, the second-highest number of "plus" signs.*** Tell the students that this is their opportunity cost.

29. Explain that **opportunity cost** is the best alternative given up when a decision is made. Tell the students to imagine they can choose one snack after school. The options are an apple, a banana or an orange. Choose a student and discuss the following:

A. How many snacks may you choose? ***One***

B. Of the three snacks, which two do you prefer? ***Answers will vary.***

C. Of the two you prefer, which would you choose to eat? ***One of the two preferred snacks***

D. By choosing to eat ______ ***(chosen snack)***, you gave up the opportunity to eat _______ ***(second choice).***

Point out that the snack given up is the student's opportunity cost. For additional practice, choose another student and repeat questions A through D.

30. Explain that any time people make a choice they give something up. Give the students the following problem:

- The school has cleared a piece of land. The principal has suggested three possible uses for the land–playground, nature trail and soccer field. The students were asked to vote on how the land should be used. The final vote was 245 students for nature trail, 200 for playground and 195 for soccer field.

31. Discuss the following:

A. What was scarce in this example? ***Land*** What does this mean? ***The school can't have all three–a playground, a nature trail and a soccer field–because there isn't enough land.***

B. What did the students have to do because of scarcity? ***Make a choice***

C. What was the decision? ***Nature trail***

D. What was the opportunity cost of using the land for the nature trail? ***Playground*** Why? ***The playground was the highest-valued alternative given up, or the second choice.***

32. Explain that in their production activity, human resources were scarce. In the school example, land was scarce. Tell the students that land is a natural resource. **Natural resources** are "gifts of nature." They are present without human intervention. Coal, sand, rocks and plants are examples of natural resources.

33. Ask the students for additional examples of natural resources. ***Answers will vary but may include trees, water, air, oil and animals.***

34. Distribute five sheets of colored paper to each group, depending on the decoration the group chose to produce. Allow time for the students to produce 10 decorations. Have the students write an economic term learned in the lesson (human resource, natural resource, scarcity, opportunity cost) on each decoration.

35. Hang the decorations in the classroom.

CLOSURE

36. Use the following questions to review the key points of the lesson:

A. What are human resources? ***People doing physical and mental work to produce a good or service***

B. A teacher and a contractor are human resources. Explain why. ***They work to produce a good or service.***

C. What are natural resources? ***Gifts of***

nature that are present without human intervention

D. Which of the following is a natural resource–oil or a pencil? ***Oil*** Explain why. ***Oil is a gift of nature and is present in the ground without human intervention. A pencil is a good made by people.***

E. What is scarcity? ***The condition of not having enough resources to produce everything people want***

F. What is scarce when five classrooms want to use the gymnasium for indoor recess and there is room for only three classrooms? ***Space in the gymnasium***

G. What is opportunity cost? ***The highest-valued alternative given up when a choice is made***

H. Mark has two possible things to do on Saturday afternoon, go to a movie or go to a ballgame with a friend. He chooses to go to the movie. What is his opportunity cost? ***The ballgame***

ASSESSMENT

Distribute a copy of Activity 2.4 to each student. Instruct the students to complete the assessment. Review answers with the students.

Answers:

1. What is scarce for the class? ***Buses for the field trips***

2. Rate the field trips from 1 to 3, with a "1" being the trip that would be your first choice for the class. ***Answers will vary.***

3. What field trip do you think the class should select? ***Answers will vary.***

4. What is the opportunity cost of your decision? ***Answers will vary, but the opportunity cost should be only one OR the other of the two remaining options.***

5. Explain why this is your opportunity cost. ***The opportunity cost is the highest-valued or best choice I gave up.***

6. How did scarcity affect the ability of the class to take field trips? ***The class couldn't take as many field trips as it wanted. The class had to choose one field trip because of scarcity.***

Visual 2.1 - **Production Instructions**

✓ Cut out the pattern for each decoration from Activity 2.1.

✓ Make sure the pattern has smooth edges.

✓ Trace the pattern on colored paper as follows:

- ✎ Yellow for the school bus
- ✎ Tan for the pencil
- ✎ Green for the scissors
- ✎ Black for the globe

✓ Cut out 10 of each product.

Visual 2.2 - **Decision-Making Grid**

Problem____

Alternatives	Criteria					
	Easy To Cut Out	Represents The Theme	Space For Words Or Drawings	Interesting To Look At		Net Value
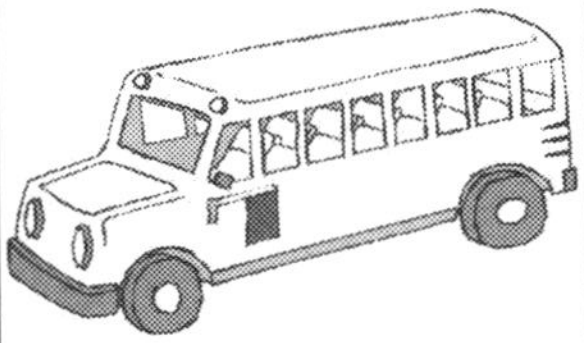						

Visual 2.3 - **Blank Decision-Making Grid**

Problem____

Alternatives	Criteria					
						Net Value

Activity 2.1 - **Patterns**

Activity 2.1 - (continued) **Patterns**

Activity 2.2 - **Decision-Making Grid**

Problem ______________________________

Alternatives	Criteria					
	Easy To Cut Out	Represents The Theme	Space For Words Or Drawings	Interesting To Look At		Net Value

Activity 2.3 - **Blank Decision-Making Grid**

Problem____

	Criteria					
Alternatives						Net Value

Activity 2.4 - **Assessment**

A fourth-grade class has three field trips planned. They are going to a theme park, the zoo and a museum. The principal announces there are only enough buses available for one field trip.

1. What is scarce for the class?

2. Rate the field trips from 1 to 3 with a "1" being the trip that would be your first choice for the class.

_____ **Theme park**

_____ **Zoo**

_____ **Museum**

3. What field trip do you think the class should select?

Activity 2.4 - (continued) **Assessment**

4. **What is the opportunity cost of your decision?**

5. **Explain why this is your opportunity cost.**

6. **How did scarcity affect the ability of the class to take field trips?**

Lesson 3 - **We've Got Goods**

LESSON DESCRIPTION

In this lesson, the students read about an elementary student and identify the goods and services she uses in a day. After categorizing goods and services as those that are privately produced or that are provided by government, the students work in groups to write their own stories. After each group writes a paragraph, the groups exchange stories, writing additional paragraphs and identifying the goods and services in each story as privately produced or government-provided.

CONCEPTS

Government-provided goods and services
Private goods and services
Taxes

CONTENT STANDARD

Standard 16 – Role of government

- **Benchmark 1 for 4th grade:** Governments provide certain kinds of goods and services in a market economy.
- **Benchmark 2 for 4th grade:** Governments pay for the goods and services they use or provide by taxing or borrowing from the people.

OBJECTIVES

The students will:

1. Distinguish between government-provided and private goods and services.

2. Explain why governments provide goods and services.

3. Explain how government pays for goods and services.

TIME REQUIRED

60-75 minutes

MATERIALS

✓ One copy of Activity 3.1 for each student
✓ One copy of Activity 3.2, cut apart to provide a card for each group
✓ One sticky note for each student
✓ One sheet of writing paper for each group
✓ One piece of drawing paper for each student
✓ Masking tape

PROCEDURE

1. Ask the students for examples of goods and services that they or their families have recently consumed. Give each student a sticky note. Ask the students to write one good or service they have used on the note.

2. Have the students place their sticky notes on the board under the heading "Goods and Services We Consume."

3. Distribute a copy of Activity 3.1 to each student. Tell the students to read the story "A Day in the Life of Maxine" and underline all the goods and services mentioned in the story.

4. Write "Goods and Services" on the board. Under that heading, create two columns, labeled "A" and "B." Ask the students for examples of the goods and services Maxine used or learned about on the field trip. Record the answers on the board under the appropriate column. Column "A" represents private goods and services. ***Alarm clock, clothes, cereal, toast, juice, lunch, book bag, play, dry cleaning, haircut, car, home, video game, book and bed*** Column "B" represents goods and services provided by government. ***Crossing guard, sidewalk,***

street, school bus, Southern Elementary School, fire station, recycling center, state park, civic auditorium, public library, traffic light and police officer

5. Tell the students that some of the goods and services on the lists are produced by private businesses and sold to consumers. These are called **private goods**. Ask the students which column represents these goods and services. *Column A* Label column "A"with the label "Private."

6. Explain that the items in column "A"are examples of private goods and services. Only the individuals who pay for the goods and services benefit from them. Discuss the following:

   A. Who paid for the breakfast cereal? *Maxine or her parents*

   B. Who benefited from the cereal? *Maxine*

   C. Was Maxine's haircut free? *No*

   D. Who benefited from Maxine getting a haircut? *Mostly Maxine, perhaps also her mother–less embarrassment*

   E. Was Maxine's book free? *No*

   F. Who benefited from the book? *Maxine*

7. Ask the students who provides the goods and services in Column "B." *Government* Label column "B" with the label "Government-Provided." Explain that **government-provided** goods and services are provided by government to its citizens. Discuss the following:

   A. Did Maxine have to pay to use the sidewalk? *No*

   B. Who benefits from the sidewalk? *Anyone who walks there*

   C. Did Maxine have to pay to use the public library? *No*

   D. Who benefits from the library? *Everyone who uses it*

8. Explain how government pays for the goods and services it provides.

   • People don't pay as they use sidewalks, streets, public schools, libraries or parks or to enjoy the protections of police and fire departments. As a result, people often think these goods are "free." These goods and services are not free. Governments use tax revenue to pay for these goods and services. **Taxes** are payments that individuals and businesses are required to make to governments.

   • Sometimes people do have to pay as they use government-provided goods and services. They may be required to pay a fee for some goods and services, such as tolls on highways and bridges and entrance fees into parks.

   • Some goods and services require a great deal of money to produce, such as national defense. The government sometimes doesn't receive enough money through taxes to pay for these goods and services, and will borrow money.

9. Ask the students to remove their sticky notes from the board under "Goods and Services We Consume" and replace them on the board in either the "Private" column or the "Government-Provided"column. Have the students explain their placements. Most of their examples will probably be private goods. Point out that people often take government-provided goods and services for granted. Yet, as shown by Maxine's story, they are a big part of our lives. Ask the students for additional examples of government-provided goods and services they use. *Streetlights, firefighter, public schools, some medical care*

10. Divide the students into groups of three. Distribute a card from Activity 3.2 to each group. Ask the groups to determine if their card represents a private or government-provided good or service.

11. Call on the groups to tape their good or service under one of the headings on the board. Ask the class if they agree with each group's placement and to explain why or why not. *Private goods and services: hamburger, television, bicycle, pet supplies, car repair,*

amusement park rides, house painting; government-provided: streetlights, mail service, bridge, police protection, public school, snowplowing highways, garbage collection, town hall

12. Direct the students' attention to the list of government-provided goods and services. Ask the students why government provides these. ***Answers will vary.***

13. Explain that government provides goods and services for several reasons.

- Citizens want governments to provide some goods and services that private businesses will not produce because once someone buys the goods or services, others won't buy the goods or services. Others won't buy them because they can receive the benefits without paying for the goods and services. For example, if one or two people in a neighborhood pay for a streetlight, everyone else who lives near the streetlight can benefit even though they didn't pay for it. Other examples are levees for flood protection and national defense.
- Citizens want governments to provide some goods and services because the goods and services provide benefits to many citizens, even when some citizens don't consume the goods and services. For example, government might provide flu shots at health clinics. Even though some citizens don't receive the shots, they benefit because their chances of being infected by the people receiving the shots are reduced. What are some other examples of this type of good? ***Education, fire protection, garbage collection, and so on***
- Citizens also want governments to provide some goods and services that the citizens think should be available to everyone, either free or at a reduced price. Examples are school lunches, postal service, parks and libraries. Private businesses would not be willing to provide these goods and services for free or at a reduced price.

14. Distribute a sheet of writing paper to each group. Tell the students that they are going to create their own "Day in the Life of ____________" stories. Stories should include examples of private and government-provided goods and services. Ask each group to decide on the name of an individual, pet or cartoon character they are going to write about. Have each group write an introductory paragraph and the first paragraph describing "a day in the life."

15. Ask the groups to exchange stories. Instruct them to add a second paragraph to the story they receive. Repeat this step, so that the groups add a third paragraph to the stories.

16. Have the groups exchange stories a third time. This time, each group should add a closing paragraph and should circle all the goods and services in the story that are private and underline those that are government-provided.

17. Have the groups share their stories and give examples of private and government-provided goods and services.

CLOSURE

18. Review the important content in the lesson by asking the following questions:

A. What is a private good or service? ***One that is produced by a private business and sold to consumers***

B. Who pays for private goods and services? ***Individual consumers***

C. Who benefits from private goods and services? ***Individuals who purchase them. Only the individual who purchased the good or service receives the benefit or satisfaction from it.***

D. Give examples of private goods or services. ***Shoes, socks, gloves, eye exams, ice cream cones, dry cleaning***

E. Give examples of goods and services provided by government. ***Schools, streetlights, police protection, roads, bridges, national defense, justice system***

F. How does government obtain the money to pay for these goods and services? ***By collecting taxes and fees from individuals and businesses, by borrowing***

G. What are taxes? ***Taxes are payments that individuals and businesses are required to make to governments.***

H. Why does government provide goods and services? ***Some goods and services provide benefits to those who don't actually use them. Private businesses will not provide some goods and services because once one consumer pays for the good, other consumers can use it without paying. Citizens think that some goods and services should be available at no cost or a reduced cost.***

ASSESSMENT

Distribute a sheet of drawing paper to each student. Ask the students to draw a picture of a government-provided good or service. Ask the students to explain why government provides this good or service instead of businesses and how the good or service is paid for.

Answers:
Pictures will vary. Students should explain that governments provide the good or service because:

1. ***Citizens want government to provide the good or service because private businesses will not. Private businesses won't provide the good or service because once someone buys the good or service, others won't.***

2. ***Citizens want government to provide the good or service because many people, even those who don't consume the good or service, benefit from it.***

3. ***Citizens want the government to provide the good or service because they think that the good or service should be available to everyone, either for free or at a reduced price.***

Activity 3.1 - **A Day in the Life of Maxine**

Directions: Read the story and underline all the goods and services.

Maxine is a fourth-grade student. She lives with her mother and her sister in the community of Southville. Maxine likes school and has many friends. Here's what a day in Maxine's life is like.

Maxine turns off her alarm clock and puts on her clothes. She has a breakfast of cereal, toast and juice. Grabbing her book bag and lunch, she walks along the sidewalk to school. At the corner, the crossing guard makes it safe for her to cross the street. On the other side, she waves to her friends arriving on a school bus.

Activity 3.1 - (continued) **A Day in the Life of Maxine**

Maxine and her classmates attend Southern Elementary School. Today the students are going on a field trip to learn about their community. They visit a fire station and recycling center, have lunch at a state park, and then attend a play at the city's civic auditorium.

In the evening, Maxine tells her mother she needs a ride to the public library to get a book for a report for school. On the way there, Maxine's mom stops off to pick up her dry cleaning and also takes Maxine to get a quick haircut. On the way home, Maxine's mother almost has an accident with her car, because she is unaware of a new traffic light that has been installed. A police officer reminds her to be more careful in the future.

Activity 3.1 - (continued) **A Day in the Life of Maxine**

At home, Maxine does her homework, plays a video game with her sister, and reads a book before going to bed.

Well, that's a typical day in the life of fourth-grader, Maxine. Maybe you do some of the same things that Maxine does each day. Perhaps you enjoy some of the same activities Maxine does.

Activity 3.2 - **Goods and Services Cards**

Activity 3.2 - (continued) **Goods and Services Cards**

Activity 3.2 - (continued) **Goods and Services Cards**

Activity 3.2 - (continued) **Goods and Services Cards**

Lesson 4 - **A Taxing Situation**

LESSON DESCRIPTION

In this two-part lesson, the students learn the definition of income tax, sales tax and property tax, as well as a simple formula to determine the amount of each tax. In addition, the students conduct a survey and participate in an activity to calculate the amount of taxes owed in various situations.

CONCEPTS

Income tax
Property tax
Sales tax
Taxes

CONTENT STANDARD

Standard 16 – Economic role of government

- **Benchmark 1 for 4th grade:** Governments provide certain kinds of goods and services in a market economy.
- **Benchmark 2 for 4th grade:** Governments pay for goods and services they use or provide by taxing or by borrowing from people.

OBJECTIVES

The students will:

1. Define taxes.
2. Use a simple formula to determine the amount of taxes.
3. Describe the different bases for sales, income and property taxes.
4. Describe how taxes help pay for goods and services provided by local and state governments and by the federal government.

TIME REQUIRED

Two 45- to 60-minute periods

MATERIALS

- ✓ Markers
- ✓ Visuals 4.1, 4.2, 4.3, 4.4, 4.5 and 4.6
- ✓ One copy of Activities 4.1, 4.2 and 4.4 for each student
- ✓ Copies of Activity 4.3, cut apart to provide one card for each student
- ✓ One sheet of chart paper for each student
- ✓ One calculator for each student
- ✓ Chart paper

PROCEDURE

Day 1

1. Ask the students why we have government. ***Governments make and enforce the rules under which we live in society. Governments also help provide some goods and services for their citizens.***

2. Explain that there are many goods and services provided by government. These goods and services are provided seemingly "without charge," meaning that individuals do not pay for them directly. An example is a public school. Explain that students who attend a public school arrive at school and walk through the doors each day without having to pay a fee to enter the building.

3. Display a piece of chart paper at the front of the room. Ask the students to list other goods and services provided by the government. Write the students' answers on the chart paper. ***Schools, roads, parks, hospitals, mail, police, fire departments, libraries, military***

4. Ask the students where governments get the money to pay for these goods and services. ***Answers will vary.*** Explain that **taxes** are payments that individuals and businesses are required to make to government. The tax money governments collect is used to pay for the operation of government and to pay for government-provided goods and services. Thus goods and services provided by the government are not "without charge." People pay for these goods and services with taxes.

5. Ask the students if they are aware of any taxes that they or members of their family pay. ***Sales tax, income tax, property tax***

6. Display Visual 4.1. Explain that most taxes are determined by taking a percent of some base. The equation used is "r x B = T."
   - "r" is the tax rate, or the fraction of the base people pay in tax, expressed as a percent.
   - "B" is the base, or the value of the thing that is being taxed.
   - "T" is the dollar amount of the tax.

   Explain that when people buy a good from the store, they usually pay a small fraction of the price of that good in taxes. When people own a home or other type of property, the value of the property might be taxed. The government will ask for a fraction of the value of the property to be paid in taxes. When people earn an income, they must pay a fraction of that income in taxes.

7. Display Visual 4.2. Explain that it is simple to use the equation as long as the students understand how to change a percent into a decimal. Explain that a percent sign tells us to divide the rate by 100. So "2%" tells us to divide 2 by 100, which equals .02. "One percent" becomes 1/100, or .01. As an option, explain that converting from percent to decimal requires moving the decimal point two places to the left, so "2%" becomes ".02." Complete the rest of the chart with the students.

8. Display Visual 4.3. Explain that there are three main tax bases—property, sales and income—as follows:
   - **Property tax** is a tax based on the value of a person's or business's property. The base (B) for property tax is the value of the person's or business's property. For most people, their property includes their home and the land it sits on. For most businesses, their property includes their factories and the buildings and the land they occupy. If a family has a home worth $200,000 and the property tax rate is 2%, the family would have to pay .02 x $200,000 = $4,000 each year in property tax. Paying property tax reduces the amount of income people and businesses have to spend.

     Local governments and state governments depend on the property tax they collect. Local governments are organized to provide governance and some goods and services that benefit local residents, such as a group of residents living in a city or county. Local governments provide police protection, fire protection, schools and roads. State governments provide state highways and bridges, state colleges and universities, state prisons and many other services.
   - **Sales tax** is a tax based on the price of purchased goods and services. The base for sales tax is the price of purchased goods and services. If the price of a coat is $40 and the sales tax rate is 5%, the sales tax would be .05 x $40 = $2. A consumer must pay $42 for the coat–the price of the coat plus the tax. A sales tax adds to the price of buying goods and services. Paying sales tax reduces the amount of income people have to spend.

     State governments and some local governments depend on the sales tax money they collect. State governments are organized to provide governance and some goods and services that benefit the residents in their state, such as education, highways, the justice system and aid to the poor.
   - **Income** is the money received for selling resources in the marketplace. For example, people earn income for the work they do–providing human resources. **Income tax** is a tax based on the amount of income

earned by a person or business in a year. The base for the tax is the amount of income earned. If someone earns $20,000 a year at his or her job and the income tax rate is 10%, he or she would have to pay .10 x $20,000 = $2,000 in income taxes. That leaves the person with only $18,000 to spend. An income tax reduces the amount of income people and businesses have to spend.

The federal government, most state governments, and some local governments collect income taxes. The federal government was organized to provide governance and some goods and services that benefit the residents in the entire country, such as national defense, highways, federal courts, social security, aid to the poor and health care.

9. Display Visual 4.4. Explain that the class is going to practice calculating a tax with each of the three bases: value of property, price of a good or service, and amount of income. Complete the calculations on Visual 4.4 as a class. The students may use a calculator for the equations. ***Johnson Family: $3,000; Susan: $.90, $15.90; Mr. Chen: $4,000***

10. Distribute one copy of Activity 4.1 to each student. Read through the tax information at the top of the page. Direct the students' attention to the question at the bottom of Activity 4.1. Read through the question with the students. Tell the students that today or this evening, they should ask an adult the question and record the answer. Explain that they may ask a parent, care giver, grandparent, another teacher, bus driver, and so on. Tell the students they should return the results tomorrow.

11. Review the important content of the lesson by asking the following questions:

A. Why do people pay taxes? ***So governments have money to pay for the goods and services they provide***

B. Can you give some examples of goods and services provided by the government? ***Public schools, roads, parks, hospitals, U.S. Postal Service, police, fire department, libraries, national defense, the justice system***

C. What is the formula for calculating the amount of a tax? ***r x B = T***

D. What does "r" stand for in the tax formula? ***The "r" is tax rate.***

E. What does "B" stand for in the tax formula? ***"B" is for base.***

F. What does "T" stand for in the tax formula? ***"T" is the dollar amount of the tax.***

G. What are some examples of local taxes? ***Property tax, sales tax***

H. What are some examples of state taxes? ***Sales tax, income tax***

I. What is an example of a federal government tax? ***Income tax***

J. What happens to the amount of income people and businesses have to spend on other things when they pay taxes? ***The amount they have to spend on other things is reduced.***

Day 2

12. Ask the students how many of them were able to survey an adult about taxes paid. ***Answers will vary.*** Tell the students to take out Activity 4.1, which they completed for homework. Explain that the class is going to graph the results. Display Visual 4.5 and discuss the following:

A. Raise your hand if the adult you surveyed pays property taxes. (Record answers on the graph.)

B. Raise your hand if the adult you surveyed pays sales tax. (Record answers on the graph.)

C. Raise your hand if the adult you surveyed pays income tax. (Record answers on the graph.)

13. Tell the students to refer to the information on the graph to answer the following questions:

A. How many of the adults surveyed pay property taxes? ***Answer will vary based on graph results.***

B. How many of the adults surveyed pay sales taxes? ***Answer will vary based on graph results.***

C. How many of the adults surveyed pay income taxes? ***Answer will vary based on graph results.***

D. Do more of the adults surveyed pay property taxes or sales taxes? ***Answer will vary based on graph results.***

E. Do more of the adults surveyed pay income taxes or sales taxes? ***Answer will vary based on graph results.***

F. Is there one tax most people pay? ***Because of rental situations, some people may not pay property taxes; most likely, more people pay sales tax and income tax.***

G. What would happen if government didn't collect property, sales, and/or income taxes? ***Governments wouldn't be able to provide as many goods and services as they do. For example, schools wouldn't receive money for buildings, supplies and teachers. Parks wouldn't be maintained. There would be less fire, police and military protection.***

H. When people and businesses pay taxes, what happens to the amount of income they have to spend on other things? ***It is reduced.***

14. Explain that the students will use their tax knowledge. Distribute a copy of Activity 4.2 and a card from Activity 4.3 to each student. Tell the students not to share their situation cards with others at their table or on their team. (**NOTE:** If the students sit in teams or at tables, ensure that each student at the table or in the team receives a different situation card.)

15. Explain that the students should read their cards and use the information from their card to answer the questions on Activity 4.2. Allow the students 5-10 minutes to complete this activity. For the next activity, if the students do not sit in teams or at tables, divide them into groups of 4-5 students each.

16. At the end of the allotted time explain that the students should take turns reading their situation cards and their answers to the questions on Activity 4.2 out loud to the students in their group. In this manner, students will "check" each other's work. Move from group to group to monitor the students' work.

17. When all the groups have finished, ask all of the students holding property tax situation cards to stand. Have each student standing read his or her situation card and share his or her answers to the questions on Activity 4.2 aloud. If any students are holding duplicate cards, ask those students to share, one at a time, their answers from Activity 4.2.

18. Repeat step number 17 for the sales tax cards and for the income tax cards.

19. Collect situation cards and Activity 4.2 from each student to review the students' work.

CLOSURE

20. Review the important content of the lesson by asking the following questions:

A. Why do people pay taxes? ***They are required by government to pay taxes. Governments use tax money to operate and to pay for the goods and services they provide.***

B. What are some examples of goods and services provided by the government? ***Schools, roads, parks, hospitals, mail, police, fire department, libraries and military***

C. What are some examples of local taxes? ***Property tax, sales tax, income tax***

D. What are some examples of state taxes? ***Sales tax, income tax***

E. What are some examples of federal taxes? ***Income tax***

F. What is the formula for calculating tax amounts? $r \times B = T$

G. What does "r" stand for in the tax formula? ***"r" is rate.***

H. What does "B" stand for in the tax formula? ***"B" is base.***

I. Why do some people pay certain taxes and not others? ***Some people might rent an apartment or a house and don't pay property tax. Some people may live in an area that***

doesn't charge sales tax. In some states people pay a sales tax on certain items and not on others. Some people may earn so little income that they don't pay income tax.

J. What would happen if government stopped collecting taxes? ***Schools wouldn't receive money. Parks wouldn't be maintained. There would be less fire, police and military protection.***

K. What happens to the amount of income people and businesses have to spend on goods and services when they pay taxes? ***It is reduced.***

ASSESSMENT

Distribute a copy of Activity 4.4 to each student.

Answers:

1. What is the equation for calculating tax? ***r x B = T***

2. Mr. Jones lives in a townhouse. The house and land are worth $100,000, and the property tax rate is 2%. What is the amount of property tax Mr. Jones pays each year? ***$2,000***

3. Richard is going to buy a new DVD. The price of the DVD is $20, and the sales tax rate is 5%. What is the amount of sales tax for the DVD? ***$1.00*** What is the total price Richard pays for the DVD? ***$21.00***

4. Matthew received a statement from his employer. This statement, called a W-2 Form, shows what Matthew earns in taxable income. This year he earned $50,000 in taxable income. The federal income tax rate for his income level is 15%. What is the total amount of income tax paid by Matthew? ***$7,500*** How much money does he have left to spend? ***$42,500.***

5. Why do people and businesses pay taxes? ***Government requires people and businesses to pay taxes.***

6. Why does government collect taxes? ***So it can pay to operate the government and pay for the goods and services government provides***

Visual 4.1 - **The Base of Tax**

Most taxes are determined by taking a percentage of some base.

This simple equation is:

$$r \times B = T$$

r is the tax rate
B is the base for the tax
T is the amount of tax

Visual 4.2 - **The Rate of Tax**

Calculating taxes by using the equation "r x B = T" is easy as long as you know how to change a percent into a decimal. To change the percent to a decimal, move the decimal point two places to the left. For example, 1% becomes .01, and 2% becomes .02.

Percentage	Decimal
1%	.01
2%	.02
3%	.03
4%	
5%	
6%	
7%	
8%	
9%	
10%	
11%	
12%	
13%	
14%	
15%	
16%	
17%	
18%	
19%	
20%	

Visual 4.3 - **Taxes Collected by the Government**

Tax	Base for Tax	Example	Level of Government Most Dependent on the Tax	Is This Tax Used by Other Levels of Government?
Property Tax	The value of a person's or business's property. For most people, their property is their home and the land on which their home sits. For most businesses, their property is their factories and buildings and the land those things occupy.	.02 (rate) X $200,000 (base) = $4,000 (tax)	Local Government	State Government
Sales Tax	Sales tax is based on the price of purchased goods and services. A sales tax adds to the price of buying goods and services.	.05 (rate) x $40.00 (base) = $2.00 (Tax) Coat price with tax: $42.00	State Government	Local Government
Income Tax	Income tax is based on the amount of money earned by a person or business.	.10 (rate) X $20,000 (base) = $2,000 (tax)	Federal Government	State Government

Visual 4.4 - **Calculating the Tax**

$$r \times B = T$$

Property Tax:

The Johnson family's home and land is worth $150,000. Their rate of property tax is 2% per year. What is the total tax?

rate	Base	Tax
2%	$150,000	

Sales Tax:

Susan wants to buy a new CD for $15.00. The rate of sales tax is 6%. What is the total tax? What is the total price paid for the CD?

rate	Base	Tax
6%	$15.00	

Income Tax:

Mr. Chen earns $40,000 income a year. Mr. Chen's rate of income tax is 10%. What is the total income tax paid by Mr. Chen?

rate	Base	Tax
10%	$40,000	

Visual 4.5 - **Graphing Survey Results**

Number of People Surveyed Who Pay Property Tax, Sales Tax and Income Tax

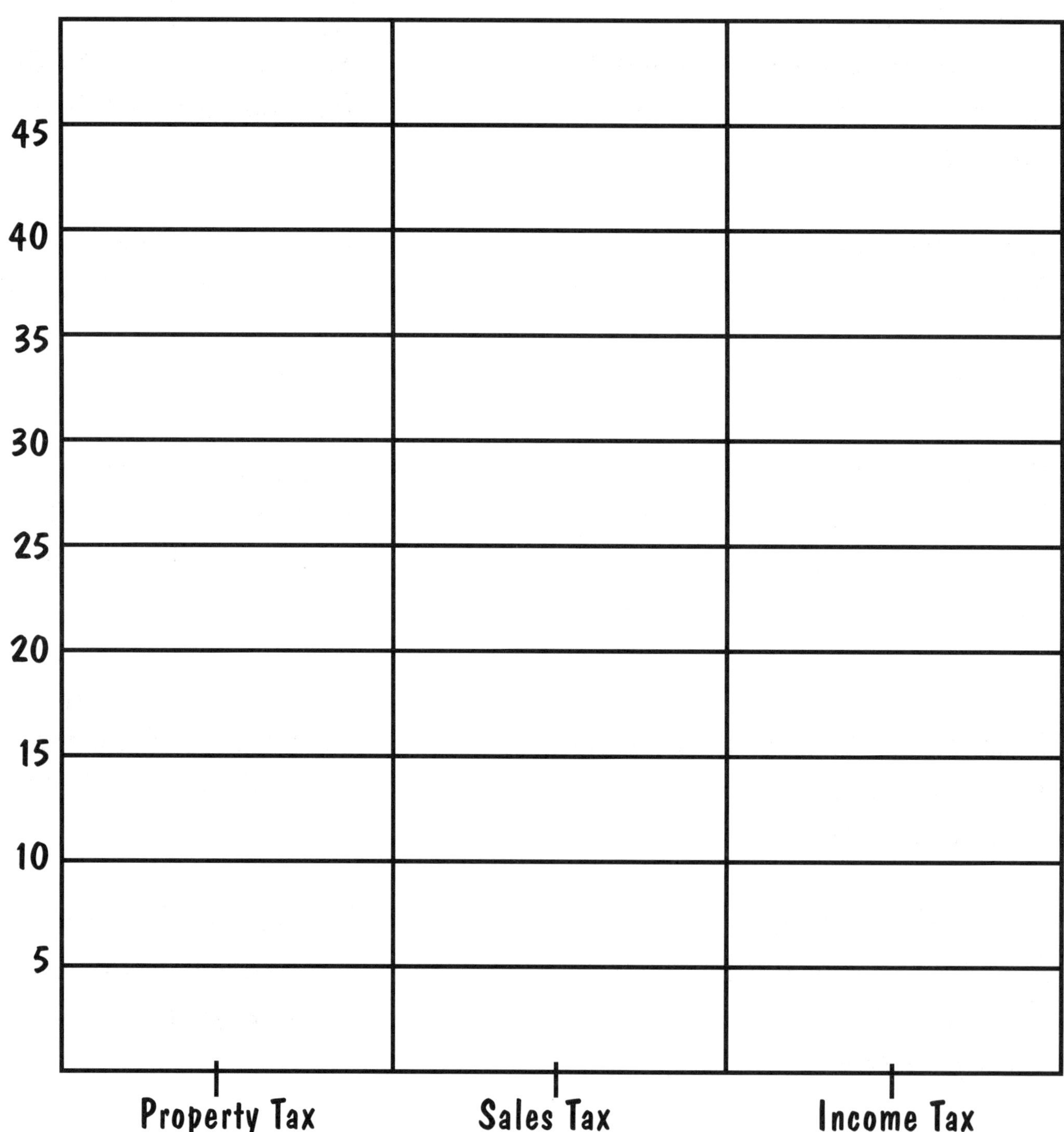

Visual 4.6 - **Taxing Situations-Answers**

Property Tax

Name: Smith
Base for tax: Value of the property
Tax rate: 1%, .01
Local government

Type of tax: Property
Base amount: $250,000
Total tax paid: $2,500

Name: Mr. Tao
Base for tax: Value of the property
Tax rate: 2%, .02
Local government

Type of tax: Property
Base amount: $10,000,000
Total tax paid: $200,000

Name: Ms. Chen
Base for tax: Value of the property
Tax rate: 2%, .02
Local government

Type of tax: Property
Base amount: $100,000
Total tax paid: $2,000

Name: Kline
Base for tax: Value of the property
Tax rate: 3%, .03
Local government

Type of tax: Property
Base amount: $750,000
Total tax paid: $22,500

Name: Mr. Johnson
Base for tax: Value of the property
Tax rate: 2%, .02
Local government

Type of tax: Property
Base amount: $150,000
Total tax paid: $3,000

Visual 4.6 - (continued) **Taxing Situations-Answers**

Sales Tax

Name: Julia
Base for tax: Price of the goods purchased
Tax rate: 5%, .05
State or local government

Type of tax: Sales
Base amount: $95
Total tax paid: $4.75

Name: Philip
Base for tax: Price of the car
Tax rate: 5%, .05
State or local government

Type of tax: Sales
Base amount: $7,000
Total tax paid: $350

Name: Jimingez
Base for tax: Price of the furniture
Tax rate: 7%, .07
State or local government

Type of tax: Sales
Base amount: $2,000
Total tax paid: $140

Name: Michelle
Base for tax: Price of the groceries
Tax rate: 7%, .07
State or local government

Type of tax: Sales
Base amount: $100
Total tax paid: $7.00

Name: Tyrell
Base for tax: Price of car wash
Tax rate: 6%, .06
State or local government

Type of tax: Sales
Base amount: $9.00
Total tax paid: $.54

Visual 4.6 - (continued) **Taxing Situations-Answers**

Income Tax

Name: Roberto
Base for tax: Taxable income
Tax rate: 15%, .15
Federal government

Type of tax: Income
Base amount: $45,000
Total tax paid: $6,750

Name: Shanelle
Base for tax: Taxable income
Tax rate: 10%, .10
Federal government

Type of tax: Income
Base amount: $350
Total tax paid: $35.00

Name: Michael
Base for tax: Taxable income
Tax rate: 15%, .15
Federal government

Type of tax: Income
Base amount: $50,000
Total tax paid: $7,500

Name: Emma
Base for tax: Taxable income
Tax rate: 10%, .10
Federal government

Type of tax: Income
Base amount: $16,000
Total tax paid: $1,600

Name: Scott
Base for tax: Taxable income
Tax rate; 20%, .20
Federal government

Type of tax: Income
Base amount: $1,000
Total tax paid: $200

Activity 4.1 - A Taxing Situation

Taxes Collected by the Government

Local Government	State Government	Federal Government
Property tax is based on the value of a person's or business's property. A property tax reduces the amount of income people and businesses have to spend.	*Sales tax* is based on the price of purchased goods and services. A sales tax adds to the price paid for goods and services. A sales tax reduces the amount of income people and businesses have to spend.	*Income tax* is based on the amount of income earned by a person or business. An income tax reduces the amount of income people and businesses have to spend.

$$r \times B = T$$

Listed above are taxes paid to the local, state and federal government. Which taxes do you pay?

____

____

Activity 4.2 - **A Taxing Situation**

Name_____________________ Date_______________________

After reading your situation card, answer the questions below.

1. Name of family or person	
2. Type of tax	
3. Base for the tax and base amount	
4. Tax rate in percent and tax rate in decimal	
5. Amount of tax paid by person or family	
6. Most likely a local, state or federal tax	

Activity 4.3 - **A Taxing Situation - Property Tax Cards**

The Smith family owns a home in a Midwest farming community. The home sits on a 100-acre farm. The tax rate is 1%, and the home and land are worth $250,000.

Mr. Tao owns an apartment building in a large city. The building is 15 stories tall and has 60 apartments. Mr. Tao's family lives in one of the apartments and rents out the remaining apartments to other families. Mr. Tao's tax rate is 2%, and the apartment building and land are worth $10,000,000.

Ms. Chen is a single businesswoman. She lives in a townhouse in the suburbs of a large city. The tax rate is 2%, and the home and land are worth $100,000.

The Kline family owns a large home on the West Coast of the United States. Their home sits on a piece of property overlooking the Pacific Ocean. The home includes 500 feet of waterfront access. The tax rate is 3%, and the home and land are worth $750,000.

Mr. Johnson, a single father with two children, owns a three-bedroom home in the southern United States. The home is located next to a good elementary school. Mr. Johnson's children enjoy walking to and from school. The tax rate is 2%, and the home and land are worth $150,000.

Activity 4.3 - (continued) **A Taxing Situation - Sales Tax Cards**

Julia received $100 from her grandmother for her birthday. She went shopping and decided to by a CD player, two CDs and a pair of jeans. The CD player is $40, the CDs are $30 and the jeans are $25, for a total of $95. The tax rate is 5%.

Philip had been saving money for many years so that he could buy a car when he turned 16. On his birthday he withdrew $7,500 from the bank. Philip found a car for $7,000. The tax rate is 5%.

The Jimingez family went shopping for new furniture. They wanted to purchase a couch, loveseat and recliner for their family room. They found a lovely set, with a price tag of $2,000, at a local furniture store. The tax rate is 7%.

Michelle went grocery shopping with her mom. Her mom filled a grocery cart with food, cleaning supplies, school supplies, books and a magazine. Michelle watched as the cashier scanned items from the cart. The groceries totaled $100. The tax rate is 7%.

Tyrell drove his dirty car to the new Water Works Car Wash. The sign advertised three types of washes. Tyrell selected "The Works," advertised for $9.00 + tax. The tax rate is 6%.

Activity 4.3 - (continued) **A Taxing Situation - Income Tax Cards**

Each year Roberto receives a statement from his employer. This statement, called a W-2 Form, shows what Roberto earns in taxable income. This year Roberto earned $45,000 in taxable income. The federal income tax rate for his income level is 15%.
Shanelle just landed her first job at a neighborhood convenience store. Shanelle calculated that if she worked 25 hours a week for $7.00 an hour, she would earn $350 every two weeks. The federal income tax rate for her income level is 10%. Answer the questions on your handout based on Shanelle's two-week income of $350.
Michael received a statement from his employer. This statement, called a W-2 Form, shows what Michael earns in taxable income. This year he earned $50,000 in taxable income. The federal income tax rate for his income level was 15%.
Each year Emma receives a statement from her employer. This statement, called a W-2 Form, shows what Emma earns in taxable income. This year Emma earned $16,000 in taxable income. The federal income tax rate for her income level is 10%.
Every two weeks Scott receives a paycheck from his employer. The most recent paycheck shows that Scott earned $1,000. The federal income tax rate for his income level is 20%. Answer the questions on your handout based on Scott's two-week income of $1,000.

Activity 4.4 - **Assessment**

Answer the following questions. You may use a calculator. Show your work.

1. **What is the equation for calculating tax?**

2. **Mr. Jones lives in a townhouse. The house and land are worth $100,000, and the property tax rate is 2%. What is the amount of property tax Mr. Jones pays each year?**

3. **Richard is going to buy a new DVD. The price of the DVD is $20, and the sales tax rate is 5%. What is the amount of sales tax for the DVD? What is the total price Richard pays for the DVD?**

Activity 4.4 - (continued) **Assessment**

4. Matthew received a statement from his employer. This statement, called a W-2 Form, shows what Matthew earns in taxable income. This year he earned $50,000 in taxable income. The federal income tax rate for his income level is 15%. What is the total amount of income tax paid by Matthew? How much money does he have left to spend?

5. Why do people and businesses pay taxes?

6. Why does the government collect taxes?

Lesson 5 - **Flagging Profits**

LESSON DESCRIPTION

In this lesson, the students work in groups to produce flags. Each group determines the total cost of its resources and intermediate goods and the unit cost of its flag. Then each group draws a card that determines the selling price for its flags. Using this information, the groups determine if they earned a profit or a loss.

CONCEPTS

Capital goods (resources)
Human resources
Intermediate goods
Loss
Natural resources
Profit
Total cost
Total revenue
Unit cost

CONTENT STANDARD

Standard 1 – Scarcity

- **Benchmark 10 for 4th grade:** Natural resources, such as land, are "gifts of nature"; they are present without human intervention.
- **Benchmark 11 for 4th grade:** Human resources are the quantity and quality of human effort directed toward producing goods and services.
- **Benchmark 12 for 4th grade:** Capital goods (resources) are goods produced and used to make other goods and services.

Standard 14 – Profit and the Entrepreneur

- **Benchmark 3 for 8th grade:** Entrepreneurs and other sellers earn profits when buyers purchase the products they sell at prices high enough to cover the costs of production.
- **Benchmark 4 for 8th grade:** Entrepreneurs and other sellers incur losses when buyers do not purchase the products they sell at prices high enough to cover the costs of production.

OBJECTIVES

The students will:

1. Define total revenue, total cost and profit.
2. Determine the total revenue and total cost of producing and selling a specific quantity of a product.
3. Analyze simple revenue and cost statements to determine if a producer made a profit or a loss.

TIME REQUIRED

60-75 minutes

MATERIALS

✓ Visuals 5.1, 5.2 and 5.3
✓ One copy of Activities 5.1 and 5.2 for each group
✓ One copy of Activity 5.3, cut apart
✓ One copy of Activities 5.4 and 5.5 for each student
✓ One small brown bag
✓ Teacher-made flag
- 1/4 piece of white or blue 9"-by-12" construction paper, stapled to a straw, using three staples. Attach a feather to construction paper on same side of paper as straw.
- Attach seven red, gold and silver self-sticking stars on the flag, and draw colored tails with colored markers on each star.

✓ Supplies for flags, such as drinking straws, coffee stirrers, felt, construction paper, stapler, staples, tape, feathers, stickers, sequins, yarn and glue

PROCEDURE

1. Hold up the teacher-made flag. Tell the students that this flag is one that could be used for a patriotic holiday. It is called the "Patriotic Dazzle Flag." Ask the students what was needed to produce this flag. Write the list of items on the board. ***Construction paper, drinking straw, stapler, staples, one feather, three markers, scissors, seven stars, table or workspace, building, workers***

2. Tell the students that every producer must buy resources to make a good or service. Review the three types of resources with the students, as follows:

   • **Capital resources** (goods) are produced goods that are used in the production process. Ask the students which of the things used to make the teacher-made flag are capital resources. ***Stapler, table, building, markers, scissors***

   • **Human resources** are the quantity and quality of human effort used to produce a product. Ask the students which of the resources used to make flags are human resources. ***Workers***

   • **Natural resources** are resources found naturally in or on the earth. Natural resources are "gifts of nature" that exist without human intervention, such as water, trees, plants and animals. Natural resources were not directly used in the production of the teacher-made flag. For example, the paper was made from trees.

3. Explain that the other items listed on the board do not fit into one of the three resource categories. These are called **intermediate goods**. These are the materials that make up the good produced (staples, construction paper, straws, feathers, stars). (**NOTE:** Both capital resources and intermediate goods are goods that are produced in order to produce other goods. Producing both capital resources and intermediate goods requires human, capital and natural resources. The difference between capital resources and intermediate goods is the role they play in producing those other goods. Capital resources provide productive services. They are the actors in the process–the tools. Intermediate goods provide the materials with which the goods are produced. They are acted upon–they are the stuff from which the goods are made.)

4. Display Visual 5.1. Point out that this is a price list for intermediate goods, capital resources and human resources that could be used to produce flags. (**NOTE:** The list will vary, depending on the type of resources available to the students.)

5. Divide the students into groups of four. Give each group a copy of Activity 5.1. Instruct the groups to use the price list to determine the total cost of producing eight of the "Patriotic Dazzle Flags." Define **total cost** as the cost of all capital resources, natural resources, human resources and intermediate goods used to produce a product.

6. Ask the students how much it cost to produce eight teacher-made flags. ***$3.84–50 cents for construction paper, 40 cents for straws, 72 cents for feathers, 13 cents for time using the stapler, 24 cents for staples, 25 cents for workspace, 25 cents for the worker, $1.12 for stars, 15 cents for markers, and 8 cents for scissors.*** Explain that this is the total cost for producing flags.

7. Ask the students if they know how to compute the cost of producing one "Patriotic Dazzle Flag." ***Answers will vary.*** Explain that to answer the question, the students must divide the total cost by eight. ***$0.48*** Tell the students that this is called the **unit cost**, or the cost of all natural resources, human resources, capital resources and intermediate goods used to produce a single product.

8. Distribute a copy of Activity 5.2 to each group. Tell the groups that they are going to design and produce their own flags. They should name their product, determine the to-

tal cost to produce eight flags, determine the unit cost and record the data in step 1 of Activity 5.2. (**NOTE:** In this lesson, the students are given the freedom to select the type of flag they want to produce. However, the students could be assigned to produce a specific flag, such as a flag for a particular country or state.)

9. Allow the group members to select the materials they want to use to produce their flags. Allow 10 minutes for production.

10. Display Visual 5.2. Record the product name for the teacher-made flag, "Patriotic Dazzle." Record the total cost for eight flags and the unit cost. Have the students share their flags, giving the product name, total cost and unit cost. Record the information on Visual 5.2.

11. Tell the students that once a product is made, the producer wants to sell it in the marketplace. Tell the students to look at the unit cost for each flag. Discuss the following questions:

A. At what price might the producers want to sell their flags? ***A price higher than the cost to produce one flag***

B. Why would producers want to sell their product at a price higher than the amount it cost to produce a flag? ***To make more money than the amount of money that they had to spend to buy the resources used***

12. Explain that when producers are able to sell a product at a price above what it cost to produce, they make a profit. **Profit** is the amount a producer has left once he or she pays the costs of producing the product. Profit provides an incentive for producers to produce the goods and services people want, and to produce efficiently. Tell the students that if the selling price for a product is below the unit cost for producing the product, the producer has a **loss**.

13. Explain that producers want to sell their products for a price higher than their costs to produce the products. However, when the product comes to the marketplace, the price might change, depending on how many producers are selling similar products or how much consumers are willing to pay.

14. Shuffle the price cards from Activity 5.3 and place the cards in the brown paper bag. Ask a member of each group to select one card. Tell the students that the price of flags has been established by the market, and that this is the price on their group's card. Explain that they can sell all eight of their flags at this price.

15. Refer the students to Visual 5.2. Record the selling price for each group. Tell the students that the money received for selling the flags is called "total revenue." **Total revenue** is the number of units sold, multiplied by the price of a product.

16. Demonstrate how to determine total revenue for "Patriotic Dazzle Flags." Have the groups determine their total revenue by multiplying the total number sold by the selling price and record the data in step 2 of Activity 5.2. Have the groups report their total revenue, and record the data on Visual 5.2.

17. Display Visual 5.3, Box "A." Explain that when total revenue is greater than total cost, the producer earns a profit. If total revenue is less than total cost, the producer experiences a loss. Point out the total revenue and total cost figures for "Patriotic Dazzle Flags." Ask the students if the producer made a profit or a loss. ***Answers will vary, depending on what price has been assigned to Patriotic Dazzle Flags by the price cards.***

18. Refer the students to Visual 5.3, Box "B." Demonstrate for the students how to compute the dollar amount of the profit or loss for Patriotic Dazzle Flags.

19. Ask the groups to complete steps 3-5 of Activity 5.2. Have the groups report the amount of their profit or loss, and record their answers on Visual 5.2. Discuss the following questions:

A. Which groups had a profit? ***Answers will vary.*** Which group had the greatest profit? Why? ***They were able to sell their flags at a higher price than other groups, they had lower costs of production, or some combination of both reasons.***

B. Which groups had a loss? ***Answers will vary.***

C. Display a flag from a group that experienced a loss. Ask the class for specific suggestions on how they might make a profit. ***Lower their costs by using fewer resources or trying to sell for a higher price***

D. What happens to businesses if they are unable to sell their products for a profit? ***They go out of business.***

CLOSURE

20. Review the important content in the lesson by asking the following questions:

A. What is total cost? ***The cost of all natural resources, human resources, capital goods and intermediate goods used to produce a product***

B. What is total revenue? ***Money received for selling a product; the number of products sold multiplied by the selling price***

C. What is unit cost? ***The cost of all natural resources, human resources, capital goods and intermediate goods used to produce a single unit of a product; the total cost divided by the number of units produced***

21. Distribute a copy of Activity 5.4 to each student. Ask the students to work in their groups to calculate the total cost and total revenue, determine whether there is a profit or a loss, and calculate the amount of the profit or loss. ***Total cost $1.30, total revenue $1.80, profit $0.50***

22. Ask the students what the profit or loss would be if the selling price were $0.08. ***Loss of $0.34***

ASSESSMENT

Distribute a copy of Activity 5.5 to each student. Review the directions with the class.

Answers:
Your friend plans to sell Play Clay at the school fair for $0.20 per container. He's not sure if this is the price he should charge to make a profit. What advice would you give him? Explain. Include your calculations.

Friend will not make a profit. His total costs are $2.71, and his total revenue at $0.20 will be $2.00. He will have a loss of $0.71. Advise selling Play Clay at $0.28 or higher per container.

Visual 5.1 - **Price List**

Item	Price
Straws	$0.05 per straw
Felt (4 flags per sheet)	$0.50 per sheet
Construction paper (4 flags per sheet)	$0.25 per sheet
Stickers	$0.03 per sticker
Rick-rack & ribbon	$0.05 per foot
Feathers	$0.09 per feather
Markers	$.05 per marker per 10 minutes
Staplers	$0.13 per stapler per 10 minutes
Staples	$0.01 per staple
Workspace	$0.25 per space per 10 minutes
Workers	$0.25 per worker per 10 minutes
Tape	$0.05 per foot
Glue	$0.01 per dollop
Colored self-sticking stars	$0.02 per star
Scissors	$0.08 per pair per 10 minutes

Visual 5.2 - **Data Sheet**

Product Name	Total Cost	Unit Cost	Selling Price	Number Sold	Total Revenue	Profit (Loss)
				8		
				8		
				8		
				8		
				8		
				8		

Visual 5.3 - **Profit or Loss**

A.

Total Revenue > Total Cost = Profit

Total Revenue < Total Cost = Loss

B.

To determine the amount of profit or loss, use the following formulas:

Total Revenue - Total Cost = Profit

Total Cost - Total Revenue = Loss

Activity 5.1 - **Cost to Produce Eight Teacher Flags**

Resources and Intermediate Goods	Cost
2 sheets of construction paper (4 flags per sheet)	
8 straws (1 per flag)	
8 feathers (1 per flag)	
1 stapler for 10 minutes	
24 staples (3 per flag)	
56 stars (7 per flag)	
3 markers for 10 minutes	
1 worker for 10 minutes	
1 workplace for 10 minutes	
1 scissor for 10 minutes	
Total	

Activity 5.2 - **Product Data Sheet**

Name of Product____________________________

Resources and Intermediate Goods	Quantity Needed to Produce Eight Flags	Price per Unit or Use	Cost of Each Resource

1. Total cost to produce eight flags: ____________________
   Unit cost: ____________

2. ____________ = ____________ X ____________
   (Total Revenue) (Number Sold) X (Selling Price)

3. Total Revenue is (> or <) Total Cost? (Circle one.)

4. Did you make a profit or a loss?

5. How much of a profit or loss did you have? Show your work here or on the back of this page.

Activity 5.3 - **Selling Price Cards**

Selling price: $0.60	Selling price: $0.70
Selling price: $0.80	Selling price: $0.90
Selling price: $1.00	Selling price: $1.10
Selling price: $1.20	Selling price: $1.30
Selling price: $1.40	Selling price: $1.50
Selling price: $1.60	Selling price: $1.70

Activity 5.4 - **Producing Glutch**

Resources and intermediate goods needed to produce glutch: Six cups of liquid starch, three teaspoons salt, three cups of white glue, 12 re-sealable plastic bags, colander for 10 minutes, bowl and spoon for 10 minutes, worker for 20 minutes, measuring cup and spoons for 10 minutes

In a small bowl, mix liquid starch with salt. Pour white glue into this mixture. Beat about 30 strokes. Pour this mixture into a colander and let it set for 10 minutes to drain the excess starch. Knead until smooth. Place small amounts into plastic re-sealable bags. Makes 12 bags.

Cost of Resources and Intermediate Goods

Liquid starch	$0.05 per cup
Salt	$0.01 per teaspoon
White glue	$0.05 per cup
Bowl and spoon	$0.10 per bowl & spoon per 10 min.
Colander	$0.10 per colander per 10 min.
Worker	$0.20 per worker for 10 min.
Plastic bag	$0.01 per plastic bag
Measuring cup and spoons	$0.10 per cup & spoon per 10 min.

Selling price per bag: $0.15

Total Cost______________________________

Total Revenue ___________________________

Amount of Profit/Loss (circle one)_______________

Activity 5.5 - **Assessment**

Resources and intermediate goods needed to produce Play Clay: Measuring cups, spoons, mixing bowl, tea kettle and stove for boiling water, five cups flour, one cup salt, four packets unsweetened drink mix, six tablespoons cooking oil, four cups boiling water, one worker for 20 minutes, 10 plastic containers

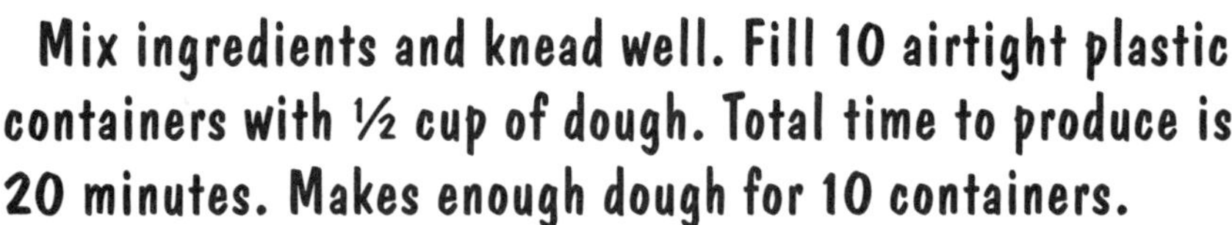

Mix ingredients and knead well. Fill 10 airtight plastic containers with ½ cup of dough. Total time to produce is 20 minutes. Makes enough dough for 10 containers.

Prices of Resources and Intermediate Goods

Flour	$0.10 per cup
Salt	$0.10 per cup
Drink mix	$0.15 per packet
Cooking oil	$0.02 per tablespoon
Measuring cups & spoons	$0.07 per cup and spoon per 20 minutes
Water	$0.03 per cup
Tea kettle and stove	$0.20 per teakettle and stove per 20 minutes
Worker	$0.25 per worker per 10 minutes
Mixing bowl	$0.10 per bowl per 20 minutes
Plastic containers	$0.04 per container

Your friend plans to sell Play Clay at the school fair for $0.20 per container. He's not sure if this is the price he should charge to make a profit. What advice would you give him? Explain. Include your calculations. Write your answers on the back of this page.

Lesson 6 - **My Problem, My Solution**

LESSON DESCRIPTION

Successful entrepreneurs recognize opportunities to solve problems. In this lesson, the students look at products that were invented to solve problems. They examine a product used to raise beds and think about why this product was invented. Divided into groups, the students then receive pictures of different products and write stories describing how they think each product came to be invented as a solution to a problem. The NCEE is grateful to Miles Kimball Company for assistance with this lesson.

CONCEPTS

Entrepreneur
Innovation
Invention
Profit
Revenue

CONTENT STANDARD

Standard 14 – Profit and the Entrepreneur

- **Benchmark 1 for 4th grade:** Entrepreneurs are individuals who are willing to take risks to develop new products and start new businesses. They recognize opportunities, enjoy working for themselves, and accept challenges.
- **Benchmark 2 for 4th grade:** An invention is a new product. Innovation is the introduction of an invention into a use that has economic value.
- **Benchmark 3 for 4th grade:** Entrepreneurs often are innovative. They attempt to solve problems by developing and marketing new or improved products.
- **Benchmark 3 for 8th grade:** Entrepreneurs and other sellers earn profits when buyers purchase the products they sell at prices high enough to cover the costs of production.

OBJECTIVES

The students will:

1. Explain and give an example of opportunity recognition.
2. Define entrepreneur, revenue and profit.
3. Explain the difference between innovation and invention.
4. Explain how profit acts as an incentive for entrepreneurs.

TIME REQUIRED

90 minutes

MATERIALS

✓ Visuals 6.1, 6.2, 6.3 and 6.4
✓ One copy of Activity 6.1, cut apart
✓ One copy of Visual 6.3, cut apart to provide a card for each group of three students
✓ Art supplies - construction paper, glue (one of each per group)
✓ Pencils
✓ Prior to start of lesson – prepare one toilet-paper tube by stuffing one half of the tube with a small amount of tissue paper or newspaper.
✓ One copy of Activity 6.2 for each student

PROCEDURE

1. Explain that department stores used to have a section called the "notions department." This department sold small items that are commonly used around the house, such as needles and thread, measuring cups, funnels and potholders.

2. Point out that today, most department stores no longer have a notions department. Ask the

students how or where people purchase notions today. ***K-Mart, Wal-Mart, Target, catalogs, online, a dollar store***

3. Display Visual 6.1. Read some of the product descriptions aloud. Explain that there is another meaning for the word "notion." A notion is an idea. Point out that the items on the list are people's ideas, or notions. These products were the ideas of entrepreneurs. Tell the students that **entrepreneurs** are people who are willing to take risks to develop new products or start businesses. They have an idea for a product, make the product and then try to sell the product.

4. Explain that if people do not buy their products, entrepreneurs fail. If people buy entrepreneurs' products, entrepreneurs receive money. They subtract all of the costs of making their products from the money they receive from selling their products. The money they receive from selling their products is called **revenue**. The revenue that is left once costs have been paid is called **profit**.

5. Explain that opportunity to earn profit as a reward is an incentive for entrepreneurs to take risks and develop new products.

6. Display Visual 6.2. Explain that the item pictured on the visual is an **invention**, and define invention as a new product. Explain that an **innovation** is an invention that has a use to people, and that inventors can earn profits from innovations. Not all inventions are innovations. If an inventor mixed water, dirt and cinnamon together, he or she might claim to have invented a "mud shake." This would be an invention, but it would not be an innovation because it would not be useful to people and would never earn a profit.

7. Explain that each item listed on Visual 6.1 was an invention that became an innovation. These products are innovations because they are useful to other people.

8. Display Visual 6.3. Explain that before these items were invented and became innovations, someone had to think of them. Explain that thinking of a new item that may be useful to people is called opportunity recognition. People often recognize opportunities for new products when they are having a problem. The new product is the solution to their problem. So opportunity recognition is the first step in solving a problem.

9. Display Visual 6.4. Tell the students this is a picture of a six-inch plastic tube. The tubes come in sets of four. The tubes are hollow plastic on one end and solid plastic on the other. Demonstrate this by showing the toilet paper tube with tissue paper or newspaper, stuffed in one half, with the other half hollow. Tell the students that all four tubes are used at the same time to solve a problem. Ask the students what the tubes might be used for. Allow time for the students to state ideas. Continue to display Visual 6.4.

10. Select three pairs of students and give each pair one of the scenario cards from Activity 6.1. Explain that each pair of students will present a story about people who had a problem. One student from each pair will read the scenario to the class while the other student in the pair acts out the action in the scenario.

11. Refer the students to Visual 6.4 and ask the students if they can think of a way the tubes might be used to solve the problems that were just demonstrated. If the students have not stated how the tubes are used, explain that the tubes are used to raise the height of a bed. The legs of the bed go in the hollow end of the tube and sit on the three-inch solid end of the tube. The bed is then three inches higher.

12. Explain that any of the people mentioned in the scenarios of Activity 6.1 could have thought of the plastic tubes. Whoever recognized this opportunity could certainly sell the tubes to people like Justin, Nicole and Loren

(the characters from the scenarios) and make a profit.

13. Tell the students to pretend that Justin was the person who thought of the solution to the problem. Ask the following questions:

A. What was Justin's problem? ***He couldn't vacuum under his bed.***

B. What opportunity did Justin recognize? ***Justin recognized that he could solve his problem if he raised his bed frame.***

C. What was Justin's invention? ***Plastic tubes***

D. Why did the invention become an innovation? ***Justin's invention was useful to people.***

E. What is the first step in creating a product that solves a problem? ***Opportunity recognition***

F. Justin recognized an opportunity, then he created the product and offered it for sale. What do we call people who do this? ***Entrepreneurs***

G. What is the incentive for entrepreneurs to do this? ***Possibility to earn profit***

14. Tell the students that they could be entrepreneurs if they recognize an opportunity. They can practice opportunity recognition by imagining how people thought of the products shown on Visual 6.3.

15. Divide the students into groups of three. Give each group a product card from the copy of Visual 6.3, a piece of construction paper and glue.

16. Instruct the students to glue the card at the top of the construction paper. Tell each group to look at the product on the card and explain that they will write a story that describes the problem a person was having when he or she thought of inventing the product. Instruct the students to write the story under the picture.

17. Choose one student from each group to present the group's product to the class. Ask the group representatives to describe the product on the group's card and tell the story the group came up with. After each presentation, ask the following questions. Answers will depend on the product and story.

A. What does this product do? ***Answers will vary.***

B. What problem was described in the story? ***Answers will vary.***

C. What is another name for the first step in creating a product that solves a problem? ***Opportunity recognition***

D. What opportunity did the person in the story recognize? ***Answers will vary.***

E. What was the person's invention? ***Answers will vary.***

F. How did the invention become an innovation? ***The students should describe the invention as being useful to people and profitable for the entrepreneur.***

G. What is another name for the person who created the product you chose? ***Entrepreneur***

H. What incentive does an entrepreneur have to do this? ***Possibility to earn profit***

CLOSURE

18. Tell the students that you will read them the following story about an invention.

The Story of Silly Putty
(adapted from The Silly Putty Story
at www.sillyputty.com)

During World War II, the United States needed rubber for truck tires and soldiers' boots, but the war made it hard to get a supply of rubber from other countries. So American scientists were asked to invent a product that could be used like rubber. James Wright, a scientist with General Electric, invented a putty that could be stretched into a long string and, when rolled into a ball, could bounce. The bouncing putty was fun, but it was not a good substitute for rubber. In fact, no one could find a use for it.

Ruth Fallgatter, a toy store owner in New Haven, CT, and Peter Hodgson, a marketing consultant, found out about the putty. They put pieces of the putty in little cases and sold them in the toy store catalog. Ms. Fallgatter lost interest in the putty, but Peter Hodgson decided to put small pieces into plastic eggs and call it Silly Putty. He took it to toy fairs and demonstrated all of the things that could be done with Silly Putty. It could be bounced like a ball. Children could make animal shapes with it. It would pick up the ink from newspaper pictures. Mr. Hodgson thought that Silly Putty would be profitable.

Mr. Hodgson sold Silly Putty all over the world. He became very wealthy. When he died in 1976, he had an estate worth $140 million.

19. Ask the students the following questions:

A. Who invented bouncing putty? ***James Wright***

B. What is an invention? ***A new product***

C. Who recognized an opportunity for using bouncing putty? ***Ruth Fallgatter and Peter Hodgson***

D. How did bouncing putty become an innovation? ***Ruth Fallgatter and Peter Hodgson demonstrated its usefulness as a toy.***

E. What is an innovation? ***An invention that has usefulness and earns a profit***

F. Who were the entrepreneurs in this example? ***Ruth Fallgatter and Peter Hodgson***

G. What incentive did Ruth Fallgatter and Peter Hodgson have for producing and selling Silly Putty? ***Possibility to earn profit***

H. Do you think Mr. Hodgson received a profit? ***Yes*** What makes you think so? ***When he died, he was very wealthy.***

ASSESSMENT

Distribute Activity 6.2. Instruct the students to work individually *(as a homework assignment)* or as a group to complete the questions.

Answers:

A. What does this item do? ***The rubber band keeps the bag from slipping into the trash can.***

B. What problem might this product have solved? ***If the bag slips into the can, garbage will be dumped on top of the bag. This would be a big mess to clean up.***

C. What is another name for the first step in creating a product that solves a problem? ***Opportunity recognition***

D. What opportunity did the person who invented this product recognize? ***The opportunity to develop a product that would secure the trash bag so it wouldn't fall in the can***

E. What was the person's invention? ***A trash can rubber band***

F. Why did the invention become an innovation? ***It became an innovation because it was useful for people and profitable for the entrepreneur.***

G. What incentive does the entrepreneur have for inventing and selling this product? ***The possibility to earn profit***

Visual 6.1 - **My Problem, My Solution**

Sipper Ice Pop Maker

Kids will remember these all their lives. Just fill with fruit juice, freeze, and you've got tasty no-mess ice pops. As the pop melts, juice drains into the base where kids 'sip' it with built-in straw. Fun for them, no mess for you. Top rack dishwasher-safe.

Butter Spreader

Love buttered corn on the cob, hate the mess? Butter Spreader glides your butter on evenly with no mess and no waste. Just add half a stick of butter, insert plunger, and push down to dispense. Curved edges neatly fit a cob of corn. Includes cap to store unused butter. White plastic.

Grip Tite

Unlike other jar openers, this one is made entirely of tough, flexible plastic, to mold itself around any lid. Hundreds of gripping teeth inside grip every inch tightly.

Butter Cutter

Slice perfect butter pats every time! Durable stainless steel wire cutter slices through hard butter or margarine sticks with ease. Cuts 1/4 lb stick at a time. Hand wash.

Ring Pull

Pull-top can rings break nails, stick, break in half, leave sharp edges. But this simple tool solves all. Just slide under ring, pull gently, can smoothly opens. For cans of soup, fruit, single-serve veggies. Non-slip, dishwasher-safe.

Visual 6.1 - (continued) **My Problem, My Solution**

Tuna Press

It slides perfectly into the top of a tuna (or salmon) can. Press with thumbs, tip out water and fatty oils. The easy result: healthier meals, no oily fingers, more fish in your dish. You can't lose! Dishwasher safe plastic.

Corn Cob Cutter

Quick, easy way to get the kernels off the cob. Stand the ear on a plate, slip the cutter over the top, and slide it down slowly; the circular blade shears all the kernels from the cob at the same time. Adjusts to fit varying diameters. Vinyl-covered handle. Metal cutter.

Carpet Cover

Prolong the life of your carpet! Simply place this polyester runner in the high traffic areas of your home and your days of expensive cleaning are over. Light-weight cover lies flat and holds securely to any carpeted surface (even stair-cases). Machine washable for easy cleanup. Made in the USA.

Top It Can Caps (TM) Set of 4

A whole 12 oz. can is sometimes too much. So just snap on this lid and the fizz will be there later. Stops spills and waste, too. You can drink and pour through the large flip cap, which features a grid for keeping wasps out. Includes 4 lids, fits standard beverage cans.

Visual 6.2 - **My Problem, My Solution**

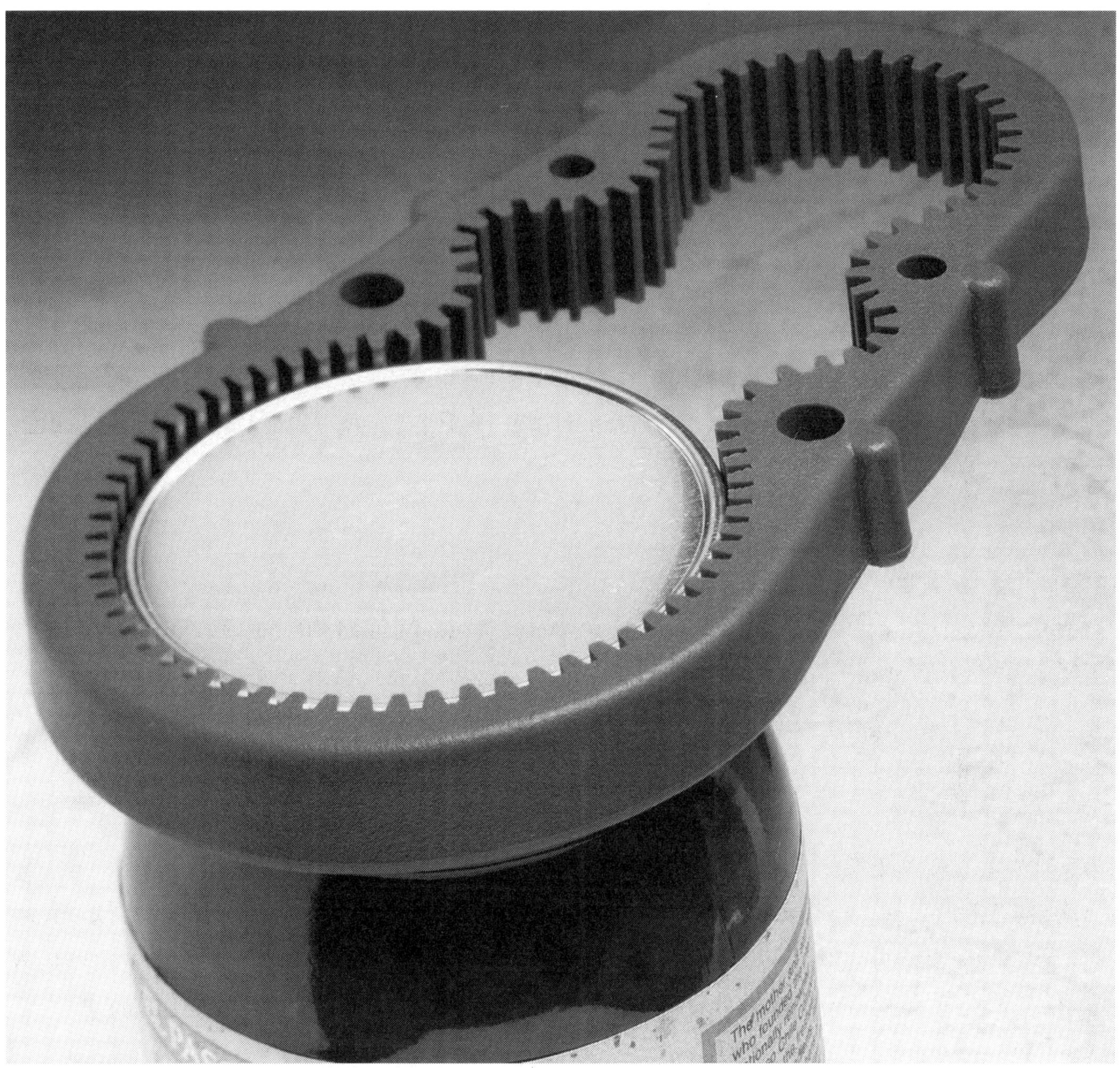

Grip Tite

Unlike other jar openers, this one is made entirely of tough, flexible plastic, to mold itself around any lid. Hundreds of gripping teeth inside grip every inch tightly.

Visual 6.3 - **My Problem, My Solution**

Top IT Can Caps™ - Set/4

A whole 12 oz. can is sometimes too much. So just snap on this lid and the fizz will be there later. Stops spills and waste, too. You can drink and pour through the large flip cap, which features a grid for keeping wasps out. Includes 4 lids, fits standard beverage cans.

Corn Cob Cutter

Quick, easy way to get the kernels off the cob. Stand the ear on a plate, slip the cutter over the top, and slide it down slowly; the circular blade shears all the kernels from the cob at the same time. Adjusts to fit varying diameters. Vinyl-covered handle. Metal cutter.

Butter Cutter

Slice perfect butter pats every time! Durable stainless steel wire cutter slices through hard butter or margarine sticks with ease. Cuts 1/4 lb stick at a time. Hand wash.

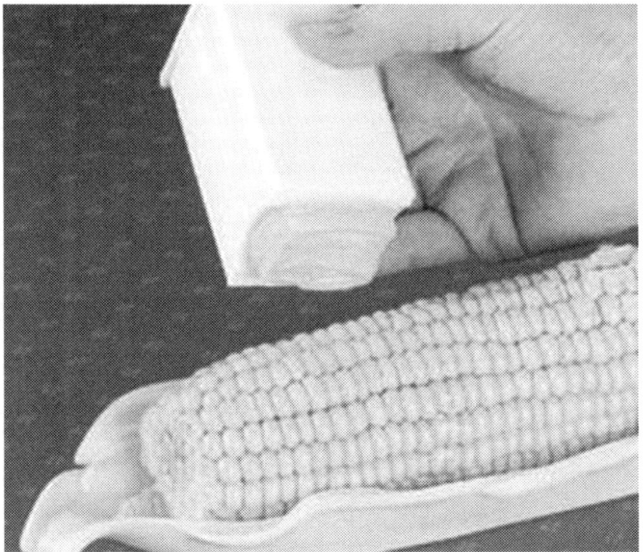

Butter Spreader

Love buttered corn on the cob, hate the mess? Butter Spreader glides your butter on evenly with no mess and no waste. Just add half a stick of butter, insert plunger, and push down to dispense. Curved edges neatly fit a cob of corn. Includes cap to store unused butter. White plastic.

Visual 6.3 - (continued) **My Problem, My Solution**

Carpet Cover

Prolong the life of your carpet! Simply place this polyester runner in the high traffic areas of your home and your days of expensive cleaning are over. Lightweight cover lies flat and holds securely to any carpeted surface (even staircases). Machine washable for easy cleanup. Made in the USA.

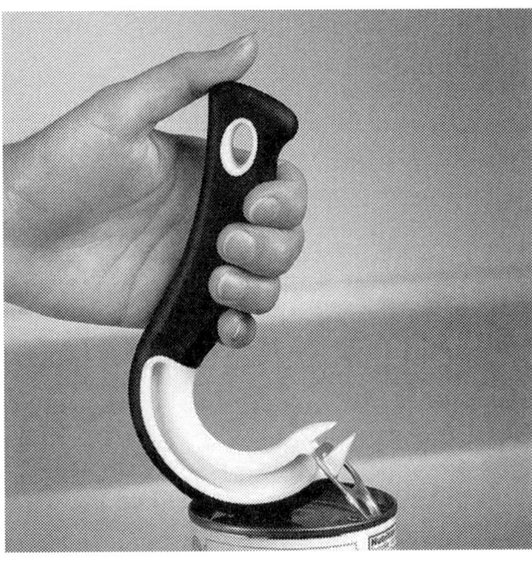

Ring Pull

Pull-top can rings break nails, stick, break in half, leave sharp edges. But this simple tool solves all. Just slide under ring, pull gently, can smoothly opens. For cans of soup, fruit, single-serve veggies. Non-slip, dishwasher-safe.

Tuna Press

It slides perfectly into the top of a tuna (or salmon) can. Press with thumbs, tip out water and fatty oils. The easy result: healthier meals, no oily fingers, more fish in your dish. You can't lose! Dishwasher safe plastic.

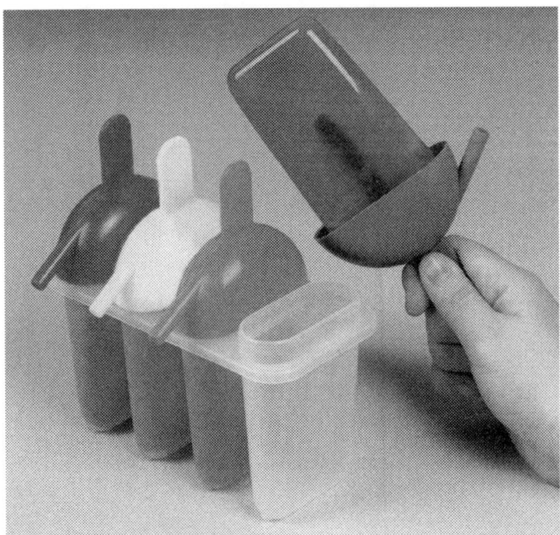

Sipper Ice Pop Maker

Kids will remember these all their lives. Just fill with fruit juice, freeze, and you've got tasty no-mess ice pops. As the pop melts, juice drains into the base where kids "sip" it with built-in straw. Fun for them, no mess for you. Top rack dishwasher-safe.

Visual 6.4 - **My Problem, My Solution**

Activity 6.1 - **My Problem, My Solution**

Scenario 1

Justin was running the vacuum in his bedroom. He lowered the handle of the vacuum to its flattest position, but the vacuum still wouldn't fit completely under his bed. He never could reach the dust that was on the floor, under the middle of his bed. As he tried to move his bed away from the wall so that he could reach under it, he scraped his arm on the plaster wall and banged his leg on the bed frame. He yelled, "Why can't they build bed frames higher?"

Scenario 2

Nicole just returned from a ski trip. She had come home three days early because she sprained her knee. She could manage to get into bed at night, but had found that it was really hard to bend her knee getting out of bed in the morning. She wished she could keep her knee straight. She said, "If this bed were three inches higher, I could hold my knee straight and get out of bed standing up."

Scenario 3

Loren loved his early 20th-century apartment. It had high ceilings, large windows and four large rooms. The only problem was that old apartments didn't have many closets, and he had sweaters and blankets he wanted to store away for the summer. He went to the store and bought some flat, plastic boxes so that he could store his winter things under his bed. After he filled all of the boxes, he tried to put them under his bed. The boxes were two inches too tall. Loren went to the hardware store to get four bricks. He placed a brick under each leg of his bed so that the bed would be taller. Then, one morning, Loren got out of bed and smashed his baby toe into one of the big bricks. He yelled, "There has to be an easier way."

Activity 6.2 - **Assessment**

Trash Can Bands - Set of 3

Heavy-duty rubber bands fit around trash cans, securing bags so you never have to reach in for messy rescue duty. Bags stay in place, keeping things tidy and utilizing their full capacity. Set of three. Fits 13 to 55 gallon cans.

Printed with permission of Miles Kimball. www.mileskimball.com 1-800-546-2255

Answer the following questions about the product in the picture.

A. What does this product do?

B. What problem might this product have solved?

C. What is another name for the first step in creating a product that solves a problem?

Activity 6.2 - (continued) **Assessment**

D. What opportunity did the person who invented this product recognize?

E. What was the person's invention?

F. Why did the invention become an innovation?

G. What incentive does the entrepreneur have for producing and selling this product?

Lesson 7 - **The Shape of Production**

LESSON DESCRIPTION

In this simulation, the students act as workers to produce two-dimensional shapes using toothpicks and marshmallows. Through the timed production process, the students learn that specialization of labor and specialization of production lead to increased productivity.

CONCEPTS

Human resources (labor)
Production
Productivity
Specialization of labor
Specialization of production

CONTENT STANDARD

Standard 6 – Specialization and Trade

- **Benchmark 1 for 4th grade:** Economic specialization occurs when people concentrate their production on fewer kinds of goods and services than they consume.
- **Benchmark 2 for 4th grade:** Division of labor occurs when the production of a good is broken down into numerous separate tasks, with different workers performing each task.
- **Benchmark 3 for 4th grade:** Specialization and division of labor usually increase the productivity of workers.

OBJECTIVES

The students will:

1. Explain the role of human resources in the production process.
2. Define specialization of labor (human resources).
3. Describe how specialization of labor is achieved through a division of labor.
4. Explain specialization of production.
5. Infer that specialization of labor and specialization of production each lead to increased productivity.

TIME REQUIRED

45-60 minutes

MATERIALS

✓ One box of toothpicks or pretzel sticks for each team of four students
✓ One bag of miniature marshmallows or small balls of modeling clay for each team of students
✓ Visuals 7.1, 7.2, 7.3, 7.4 and 7.5
✓ One copy of Activity 7.1 for each student
✓ Blank overhead transparency
✓ Overhead markers

PROCEDURE

1. Tell the students that they are going to be human resources. **Human resources** are people working to produce a good or service. People often refer to human resources as labor. In this activity, the students' job will be to produce as many copies of the shapes displayed in Visual 7.1 as possible. Display Visual 7.1. Name the shapes in Visual 7.1 and briefly describe the similarities and differences.
   - A rectangle is a four-sided figure with opposite sides that are equal in length and parallel. Rectangles have four right angles.
   - A trapezoid is a four-sided figure. Only two of the sides are parallel. Trapezoids have no right angles.
   - A rhombus is a four-sided figure. The sides are of equal length, but a rhombus has no right angles. A diamond is a type of rhombus.

- A pentagon is a five-sided figure.
- A triangle is a three-sided figure.
- A square is a four-sided figure. The sides of a square are equal. Squares have four right angles.

2. Explain that the students will use toothpicks and marshmallows to produce the shapes. Demonstrate how to produce one of the shapes.

3. Display Visual 7.2. Through discussion, help the students determine how many toothpicks and marshmallows are required to produce each shape. Write this information in the appropriate spaces on Visual 7.2. ***Square: four toothpicks and four marshmallows; Triangle: three toothpicks and three marshmallows; Pentagon: five toothpicks and five marshmallows; Trapezoid: two toothpicks for the long side, one toothpick for each remaining side, and five marshmallows; Rectangle: two toothpicks for each long side, one toothpick for each short side, and six marshmallows; Rhombus: four toothpicks and four marshmallows***

4. Divide the students into six teams (as equal-sized as is possible). Give each team one bag of marshmallows and one box of toothpicks.

Round 1

5. Instruct each student to produce one of each shape using the toothpicks. Leave Visual 7.2 on the overhead for reference. Tell the students to begin production.

6. At the end of five minutes, stop production. (**NOTE:** For older students, allow only three minutes per production round.) Most of the students will not have produced one of each shape. Display Visual 7.3 and ask each team the following questions. As teams respond, record the number of each shape produced by each team on the board or on a blank transparency. After polling each team, total the responses and record in the column titled "Round 1" on Visual 7.3.

    A. How many rectangles did your team complete? ***Answers will vary.***

    B. How many trapezoids did your team complete? ***Answers will vary.***

    C. How many rhombuses did your team complete? ***Answers will vary.***

    D. How many pentagons did your team complete? ***Answers will vary.***

    E. How many triangles did your team complete? ***Answers will vary.***

    F. How many squares did your team complete? ***Answers will vary.***

    G. What would make it easier for each member of your team to complete a model of each shape? ***More time, each person doing only part of the production***

7. Display Visual 7.4. Reveal only the term "Specialization of Labor." Read the definition of specialization of labor from the transparency. Explain that if students were producing "smiley-face" cookies and they wanted to specialize their human resources, one student might spread the icing on the cookie, a second student would place raisins on the cookie for eyes, a third student would place a raisin on for the nose, a fourth student would use a piece of licorice for the mouth and a fifth student would wrap the cookie.

8. Ask the students to discuss how they might specialize their human resources and create an assembly line for producing each shape. After the students have had time to discuss, ask each team to share its ideas. ***Some students could place marshmallows on both ends of a toothpick, other students could place a marshmallow on only one end of a toothpick, other students could join the pieces together to make the desired shape.***

Round 2

9. Tell the students that they will produce shapes using an assembly-line method. Again, they should produce as many of each shape as pos-

sible. Display Visual 7.2 again to remind the students how many toothpicks and marshmallows are required to produce each shape.

10. Allow time for the students to organize the assembly line and practice producing shapes. After the students have correctly produced one or two shapes, stop the practice and begin production.

11. Stop the assembly-line production at the end of five minutes (or three minutes for older students). Ask each team the following questions. As teams respond, record the number of each shape produced by each team on the board or on a blank transparency.

A. How many rectangles did your team complete using an assembly line? ***Answers will vary.***

B. How many trapezoids did your team complete using an assembly line? ***Answers will vary.***

C. How many rhombuses did your team complete using an assembly line? ***Answers will vary.***

D. How many pentagons did your team complete using an assembly line? ***Answers will vary.***

E. How many triangles did your team complete using an assembly line? ***Answers will vary.***

F. How many squares did your team complete using an assembly line? ***Answers will vary.***

12. Display Visual 7.3 again. Total the team responses and record the total production of each shape in the column titled "Round 2." Ask the students how specializing their human resources and working in assembly lines changed the results in Round 2, as compared with Round 1. ***More shapes were produced when working in an assembly line.***

13. Display Visual 7.4 again. Reveal the term "Productivity" and read the definition. Explain that in this activity, productivity will be measured by team rather than by worker. Explain that in each round teams had five minutes (or three minutes) to produce. Discuss the following:

- In Round 2 the teams were able to produce more shapes than they could in Round 1.
- This means that the teams were more productive in Round 2 than they were in Round 1.
- This increase in productivity occurred because the teams produced using specialization of human resources in Round 2.

14. Tell the students that the increase in productivity after Round 2 was the result of specializing the use of labor–that is, having the students concentrating on one thing and doing it well.

15. Refer back to the tally marks written on the board or transparency for Round 2. Ask the students if one team in particular made more squares than the others. ***Answers will vary.*** Ask the same question about each shape.

16. Display Visual 7.4 again. Reveal "Specialization of Production" and read the definition. Explain that people usually specialize in the production of a specific good or service. For example, doctors specialize in providing medical care, mechanics specialize in repairing cars, teachers specialize in education, and plumbers specialize in installing and repairing plumbing. Ask the students how they could specialize when producing models of each shape. Lead the discussion to the idea of having each team specialize in the production of one shape.

17. Refer back to the answers the teams gave in step 15. Given the information, discuss which team might be best suited to specialize in the production of each shape. After the discussion, assign/identify the shape each team will produce in the third round.

Round 3

18. Ask the students whether their teams can still specialize their human resources if they specialize in producing only one shape. ***Yes, each worker could be responsible for a different part of the shape the team is assigned.*** Allow the teams to discuss and decide how team members will specialize their human resources in the production of the assigned shapes.

19. Tell the students that each group will have five minutes (or three minutes) to produce as many of its assigned shape as possible. Remind the students that they should still use specialization of human resources. Display Visual 7.2 again for reference. If time permits, allow groups a few minutes to practice production. Then begin the timed production round.

20. At the end of five minutes, stop production. Display Visual 7.3 again. Ask each team how many shapes it was able to produce. As the teams respond, record their answers on Visual 7.3 in the column titled "Round 3." Discuss the following questions:

A. How do the numbers in Round 3 compare with those in Rounds 1 and 2? ***The numbers recorded for Round 3 should be greater than those recorded for Rounds 1 and 2.***

B. What is productivity? ***The amount of output produced per team in a given amount of time. If necessary, refer to Visual 7.4.***

C. Did productivity increase or decrease in Round 3? ***Increase***

D. What caused the increase in productivity? ***Specialization of labor and specialization of production***

21. Collect the shapes from the students.

CLOSURE

22. Explain that this activity shows that the specialization of labor and specialization of production leads to increased productivity.

23. Ask the students the following questions:

A. What are human resources? ***Human resources are people doing physical and mental work to produce a good or service. Human resources are workers.***

B. How were you a human resource in this activity? ***We worked to make the shapes.***

C. How did workers produce in Round 1? ***Each worker tried to make as many models of each shape as possible.***

D. Why didn't each worker complete a model of each shape in Round 1? ***Not enough time, some of the shapes were difficult to produce, and so on.***

E. What changed in Round 2? ***The human resources in each group specialized their human resources by using an assembly line to make each shape.***

F. How were human resources specialized in Round 2? ***Each human resource performed only one or two tasks in the production of a shape.***

G. Give an example of the task you performed on the assembly line for pentagons. ***Answers will vary, but might include something like: I received a marshmallow with two toothpicks in it. I added a marshmallow to the end of each toothpick.***

H. Was your team more productive in Round 1 or Round 2? Why? ***Round 2, because each worker concentrated on doing one or two things–that is, each team used specialization of labor.***

I. What happened in Round 3? ***Teams specialized in labor and production, or concentrated in producing only one shape, still using an assembly-line approach.***

J. Which round was most productive? Why? ***Round 3, because we specialized in the production of one shape and because we divided our human resources to produce multiple models of one shape.***

K. Give some examples of human resources in your community. ***Teacher, doctor, lawyer, nurse, truck driver, mechanic***

L. How do these human resources use specialization of production? ***Teachers concentrate on teaching. They do not grow their***

own food or care for their own medical problems.

M. Give examples of ways you could use specialization of labor on other school projects. ***For a group research project, one person could look up information in books or on the Internet, another person could type up the notes, another person could draw illustrations, and so on.***

ASSESSMENT

Distribute a copy of Activity 7.1 to each student. Review the directions with the students, and have them answer the questions.

Display Visual 7.5 and allow the students to check their work.

Visual 7.1 - **The Shape of Production – Shapes**

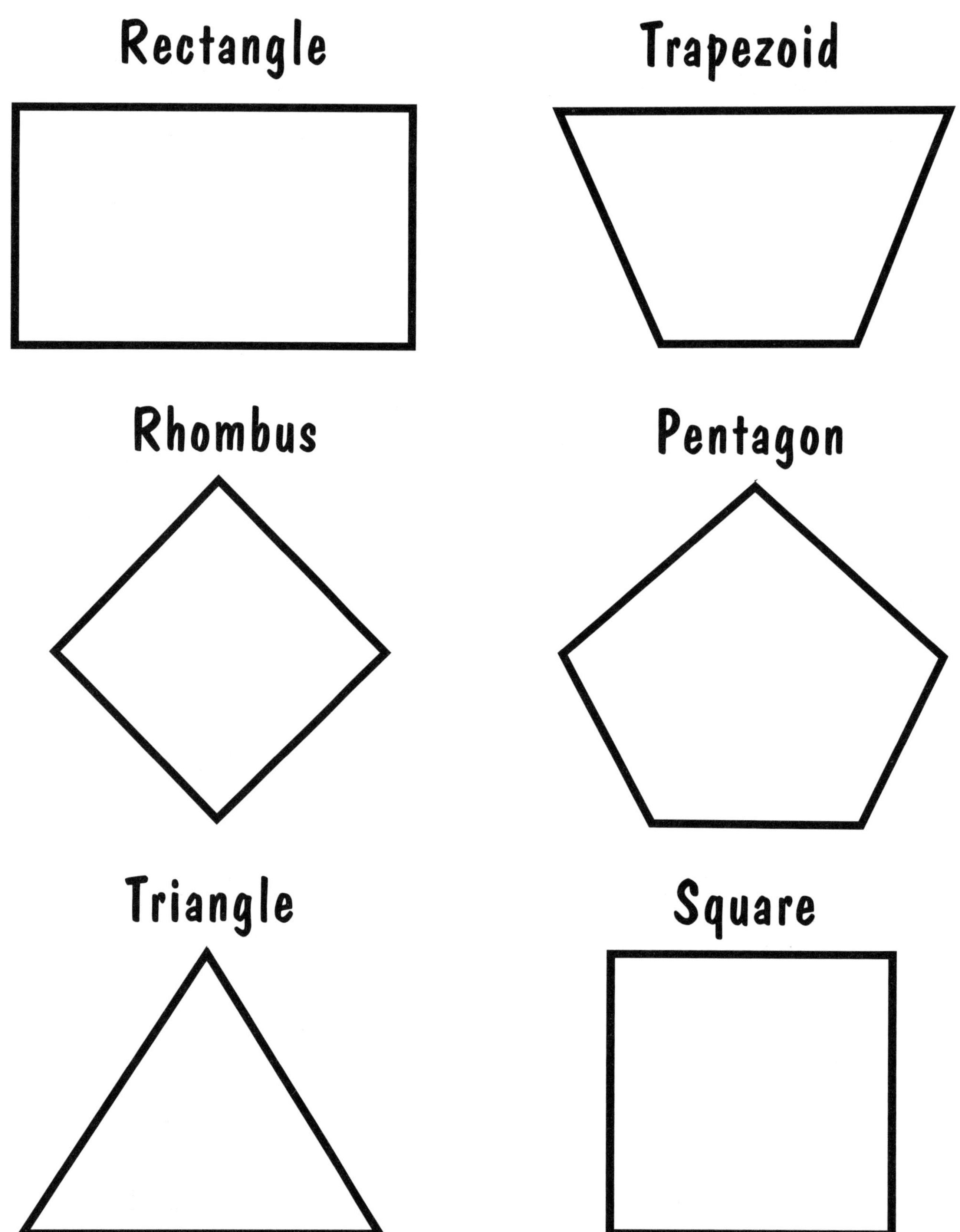

Visual 7.2 - **Supplies for Each Shape**

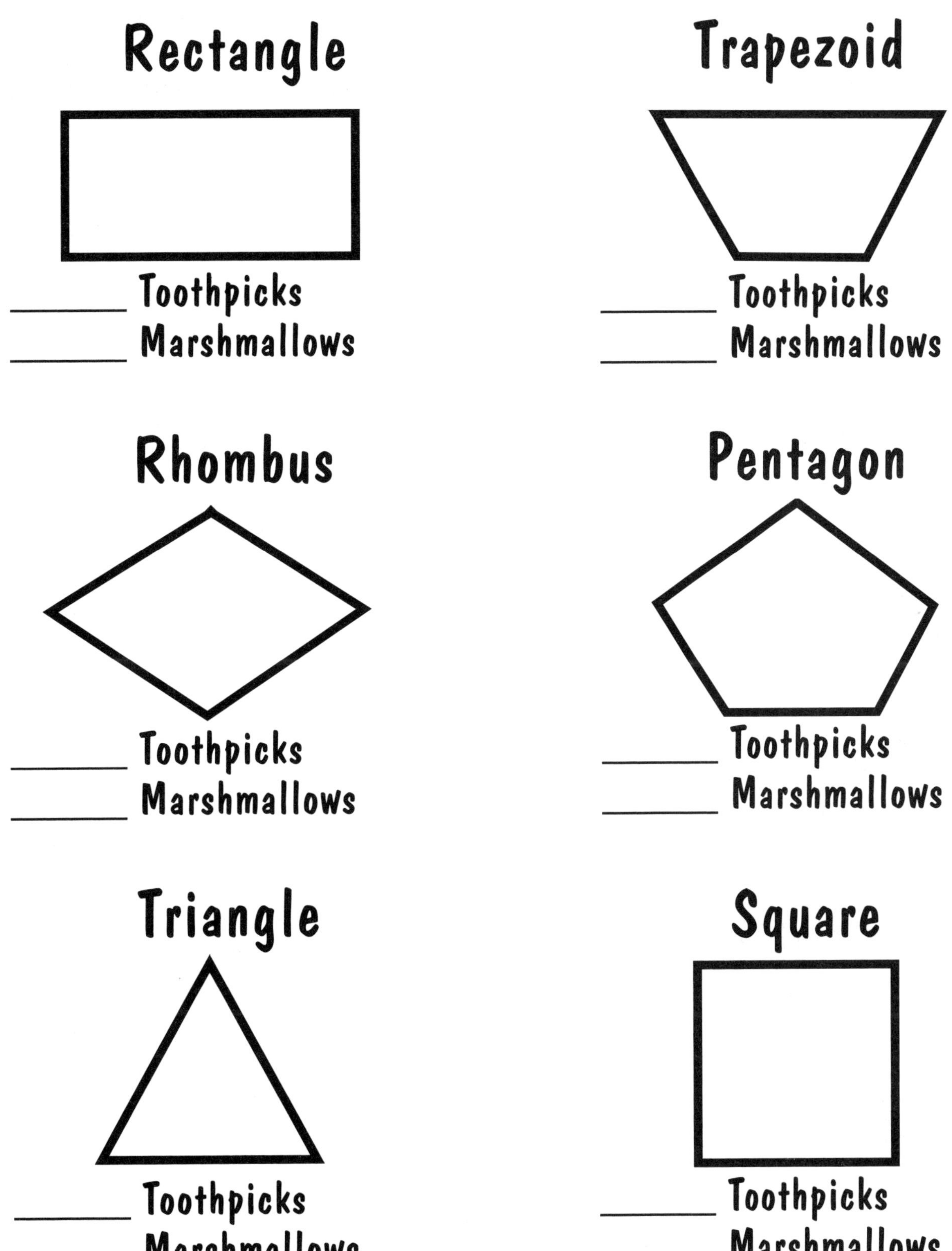

Visual 7.3 - **Production Table**

	Round 1	Round 2	Round 3
Rectangle			
Trapezoid			
Rhombus			
Pentagon			
Triangle			
Square			

Visual 7.4 - **Definition of Terms**

SPECIALIZATION OF LABOR occurs when human resources (workers) perform only a single, or very few, step(s) in the production of a product, as they do when working on an assembly line.

PRODUCTIVITY is the amount of output produced per worker in a given amount of time.

SPECIALIZATION OF PRODUCTION occurs when a group (or individual) produces a smaller range of goods and services than they consume.

Visual 7.5 - **Assessment - Answers**

For a class party, there's a lot of work to do. The classroom must be decorated, snacks prepared, and activities and games planned. Often the teacher does much of this work.

1. Who, besides the teacher, are human resources and could help get ready for the party?

   PARENT VOLUNTEERS, STUDENTS

2. List the jobs a human resource might do while making cookies as a snack for the party.

1. Measure the ingredients
2. Mix the ingredients
3. Put cookies on a baking sheet
4. Decorate cookies

Visual 7.5 - (continued) **Assessment - Answers**

3. How could the workers specialize their human resources while making cookies?

   ONE PERSON COULD MEASURE THE INGREDIENTS, ANOTHER PERSON COULD MIX THE INGREDIENTS, A THIRD PERSON COULD PUT COOKIES ON THE BAKING SHEETS, A FOURTH PERSON COULD DECORATE THE COOKIES.

4. How could parent volunteers use specialization of production to get all of the work done for the party?

   ONE OR TWO PARENTS COULD DECORATE THE CLASSROOM. ONE OR TWO PARENTS COULD MAKE THE SNACKS. ONE OR TWO PARENTS COULD PLAN GAMES. ONE OR TWO PARENTS COULD PLAN ACTIVITIES.

Activity 7.1 - **Assessment**

For a class party, there's a lot of work to do. The classroom must be decorated, snacks prepared, and activities and games planned. Often the teacher does much of this work.

1. Who, besides the teacher, are human resources and could help prepare for the party?

2. List the jobs a human resource might do while making cookies as a snack for the party.

1.
2.
3.
4.

Activity 7.1 - (continued) **Assessment**

3. **How could the workers specialize their human resources while making cookies?**

4. **How could parent volunteers use specialization of production to get all of the work done for the party?**

Lesson 8 - **Competing for Buyers**

LESSON DESCRIPTION

In this lesson, the students consider ways in which sellers compete to attract consumers to buy various products, such as hamburgers, movie rentals and cereal. Through the activities, the students recognize that consumers benefit from competition because competition results in lower prices, higher product quality, greater variety and better customer service.

CONCEPTS

Competition
Price

CONTENT STANDARD

Standard 9 – Role of Competition

- **Benchmark 2 for 4th grade:** Competition among sellers results in lower costs and prices, higher product quality and better customer service.
- **Benchmark 1 for 8th grade:** Sellers compete on the basis of price, product quality, customer service, product design and variety, and advertising.

OBJECTIVES

The students will:

1. Define price.
2. Explain that sellers compete on the basis of price, product quality, customer service, product design and variety, and advertising.
3. Give examples of competition among sellers.
4. Explain the benefits of competition to buyers.

TIME REQUIRED

45-60 minutes

MATERIALS

✓ One copy of Activity 8.1 for each group
✓ Five copies of Activity 8.2, cut apart
  • Place all hamburger cards together, all pizza cards together, and so on.
✓ Visual 8.1
✓ One copy of Activity 8.3 for each student
✓ Poster board and marker for each group
✓ Five pieces of construction paper
  • Write one of the following on each piece of construction paper: "variety and design," "quality," "advertising," "customer service" and "price."
✓ Masking tape
✓ Highlighting marker for each student

PROCEDURE

1. Introduce the activities in the lesson by writing "Pizza" on the board. Ask how many students eat pizza and how often they eat pizza. ***Answers will vary.*** Discuss the following questions:
   A. Where do you usually eat pizza? ***Home, various fast-food restaurants, other restaurants***
   B. Do you like thick pizza crust or thin pizza crust? ***Answers will vary.***
   C. What toppings do you like on your pizza? ***Answers will vary.***

2. Point out that there are many varieties of pizza available, and ask the students why they think this is the case. ***Answers will vary.***

3. Explain that the students are going to work in small groups to analyze different products.

4. Divide the class into small groups of 3-4 students each. Assign each group one of the following products: hamburgers, pizzas, haircuts, toothpaste, cereal, athletic shoes, movie rentals or gum. Distribute a copy of Activity 8.1 to each group. Review the instructions as follows:

   • List as many businesses that produce your group's product as possible. For example, if your product is hamburgers, you might list McDonald's, Wendy's and other restaurants that sell hamburgers.

   • List as many types, flavors or varieties of your group's product as you can. For example, if your product is pizza, you might list cheese, sausage, thin crust.

   • Look at the table on the second page of Activity 8.1. Place an "X" in the second column of the table next to each statement that fits your group's product. For example:

   – If your product is toothpaste and you have seen coupons that take cents off the price of toothpaste, place an "X" in the second column next to the first statement.

   – If the producer(s) of your group's product offers value meals that combine pizza and soda for a special price, place an "X" in the second column next to the second statement.

   – If the producer(s) delivers food to your home or offers some other special service, put an "X" in the second column next to the third statement.

   – If you have seen advertisements for the product on television, put an "X" in the second column next to the fourth statement.

   – If you have seen advertisements for the product in magazines, put an "X" in the second column next to the fifth statement.

   – If you have heard advertisements for the product on the radio, put an "X" in the second column next to the last statement.

   • If there's a difference between the quality of one type of your product and the quality of another type of your product, explain what the difference is. For example, if one hamburger tastes better or is bigger, one toothpaste tastes better, or one athletic shoe feels better, write that in the space available.

5. Allow time for the groups to complete their work. When the groups have completed their work, distribute a piece of poster board and a marker to each group. Instruct the groups to use the poster board to display the information about their products. Allow time for the students to work. While the students work, tape the signs (variety and design, quality, advertising, customer service and price) along the top of the chalkboard.

6. Ask the groups to tape their posters along the wall, and have a representative from each group report the group's results.

7. When the groups have completed their presentations, display Visual 8.1 and ask the following questions about each product. As students respond, enter their responses in the appropriate cell on the table.

   A. Are there different varieties of this product? ***Hamburger: yes; pizza: yes; haircuts: yes; toothpaste: yes; cereal: yes; athletic shoes: yes; movie rentals: yes; gum: yes***

   B. Do people who produce and sell this product offer special customer service? ***Hamburger: drive-through, carry-out; pizza: delivery, carry-out; haircuts: no; toothpaste: no; cereal: no; athletic shoes: no; movie rental: mail delivery, drive-up drop-off; gum: no***

   C. Do people who produce and sell this product advertise? ***Hamburgers: yes; pizza-yes; haircuts: yes; toothpaste: yes; cereal: yes; athletic shoes: yes; movie rental: yes; gum: yes***

   D. Are there differences in the quality of different brands or types of this product? ***Hamburger: yes; pizza: yes; haircuts: yes; toothpaste: yes; cereal: yes; athletic shoes: yes; movie rentals: yes; gum: yes***

   E. Are there differences in the price for this product? ***Yes, for all products***

8. Ask the students in what types of competitions they participate. ***Races, board games,***

sports games, and so on. Point out that in these situations, people compete to win the race or game.

9. Explain that sellers compete, too. Sellers are competing for buyers. Sellers compete on the basis of price, product quality, customer service, product design and variety, and advertising.

10. Explain that **price** is the amount people pay when they buy a product and the amount that sellers receive when they sell the product. Ask the students for examples of price competition. ***One business puts its product on sale. A business offers a cents-off coupon. A business offers a buy-one-get-one-free coupon.*** Point out that a cents-off coupon reduces the price of one product compared with another, a buy-one-get-one-free coupon reduces the price of one product compared with another, and putting a product on sale reduces the price of one product compared with another.

11. Tell the students to consider the posters they have seen for the various products as they answer the following questions about the non-price ways in which sellers compete:

    A. Give an example of competition based on quality. ***One type of hamburger is thicker than another, one type of toothpaste does a better job cleaning teeth.***

    B. Give an example of competition based on customer service. ***One pizza maker offers delivery, restaurants offer carry-out, a restaurant offers drive-through service, a movie rental company allows you to order online and receive and return movies via mail.***

    C. Give an example of competition based on product design and variety. ***Many types of pizzas and hamburgers, many different types of movies, many flavors and varieties of gum***

    D. Give an example of competition based on advertising. ***Ads for products on television or radio, special prizes with certain hamburger or pizza meals, billboard ads***

12. Remind the students that sellers compete to "win" buyers. Ask the students if this competition is good for buyers. ***Yes*** Discuss the following questions:

    A. What if there were only one type of hamburger available, and it was a thick hamburger on rye bread with Swiss cheese and onion? How many of you would be happy? ***Answers will vary.***

    B. What if the only type of pizza available had a thick crust with vegetable topping? How many of you would be happy? ***Answers will vary.***

    C. What if there were only one type of toothpaste available–peppermint? How many of you would be happy? ***Answers will vary.***

    D. What if you were only able to buy plain, white athletic shoes? How many of you would be happy? ***Answers will vary.***

13. Explain that buyers benefit from competition, because there is more variety. Each of us has a chance to get the kind of hamburger, pizza or athletic shoes we want because businesses offer many varieties, with different quality and different services. Another way that buyers benefit from competition is that sellers reduce prices to try to "win" buyers.

14. Explain that although lower prices tend to attract more buyers, sellers may not be able to lower their prices and still pay the cost of producing their goods. However, if they can find a way to lower their costs, then they would also be able to lower their prices. Thus in trying to attract more buyers, sellers have a strong incentive to try to lower their costs so that they can lower the price.

CLOSURE

15. Distribute the correct set of product cards to each group (hamburgers to the hamburger

group, and so on). Explain that signs are posted along the top of the chalkboard. These signs represent the ways in which sellers compete.

16. Tell the groups to discuss whether the sellers of their products compete in each of the ways listed on the chalkboard. Then the groups should tape the card for their product under the sign representing that type of competition. For example, if sellers of hamburgers compete on the basis of variety, the hamburger group should place a hamburger card under the "variety and design" sign. Allow time for the students to work. Discuss the following questions:

A. What are different ways in which sellers compete? ***Price, variety and product design, quality, customer service, and advertising***

B. Why do sellers compete? ***To win buyers, so buyers will buy the sellers' product***

C. How do buyers benefit from competition? ***More variety, lower prices, different quality, different services***

ASSESSMENT

Distribute a copy of Activity 8.3 and a highlighting marker to each student. Review the instructions.

Answers to first part of Activity – Highlight examples of sellers competing: ***Students should underline: "gave each customer a small cookie," "reduced the price of her lemonade," "putting slices of lemon in her lemonade," "began selling strawberry lemonade" and "advertising fliers."***

Answers to second part of Activity:

1. From the examples you highlighted, list the ways Dana and Joan competed ***Price: free cookie; price: lower price; quality: lemon slice; variety: strawberry lemonade; advertising: advertising fliers***

2. Dana and Joan were competing for buyers. How did the buyers benefit? ***Customers had more variety, lower price, better quality.***

Visual 8.1 - **Types of Competition**

Product	Design and Variety	Customer Service	Advertising	Quality	Price
Hamburgers					
Pizzas					
Haircuts					
Toothpaste					
Cereal					
Athletic Shoes					
Movie Rentals					
Gum					

Activity 8.1 - **Product Information**

Answer the following questions based on your group's product.

Our product is ____

1. List as many businesses that produce your product as possible.

2. List as many types, flavors or varieties of this product as you can.

Activity 8.1 - (continued) **Product Information**

3. In the chart below, put an "X" in the second column, next to the statements that apply to your product.

Sometimes producers offer coupons that reduce the price of the product (for example, 25 cents off the price of a can of soup).	
Sometimes producers offer specials such as a "value meal" or "buy a cookie and get a soda free."	
Sometimes producers of this product offer special services such as drive-through service or delivery service.	
There are advertisements for this product on television.	
There are advertisements for this product in magazines or in the newspaper.	
There are advertisements for this product on the radio.	

4. Describe any differences in the quality of these products.

Activity 8.2 - **Product Placement**

Activity 8.3 - **Assessment**

Read the story below.
Highlight examples of sellers competing.

Dana opened a lemonade stand on Tuesday. She sold six-ounce cups of lemonade for 25 cents a cup.

On Wednesday, Joan opened her lemonade stand two doors down from Dana's. Joan charged 25 cents for a six-ounce cup, too, but Joan also gave a small cookie to each customer who bought a cup of lemonade.

The next day, Dana reduced the price of her lemonade to 20 cents per cup.

The day after that, Joan began putting slices of lemon in her lemonade because it made her lemonade taste better.

Two days later, Dana began selling strawberry lemonade in addition to regular lemonade.

Three days later, Joan began putting advertising fliers in the doors of houses in the neighborhood.

Activity 8.3 - (continued) **Assessment**

Answer the following questions:

A. From the examples you highlighted, list the ways Dana and Joan competed.

____

____

____

____

____

____

B. Dana and Joan were competing for buyers. How did the buyers benefit?

____

____

____

____

____

____

Lesson 9 - **Bulletin-Board Banking**

LESSON DESCRIPTION

In this lesson, the students participate in activities that demonstrate the role of banks in a community. They learn that banks facilitate community growth by receiving funds from savers and transferring a portion of those funds to borrowers. They also learn that borrowed funds are used to buy large items such as cars and to construct new homes, buildings and factories; provide new equipment; and expand businesses in the community.

CONCEPTS

Borrowing
Income
Interest
Saving

CONTENT STANDARD

Standard 10 – Role of Economic Institutions

- **Benchmark 1 for 4th grade:** Banks are institutions where people save money and earn interest, and where other people borrow money and pay interest.
- **Benchmark 2 for 4th grade:** Saving is the part of income not spent on taxes or consumption.
- **Benchmark 1 for 8th grade:** Banks and other financial institutions channel funds from savers to borrowers and investors.

OBJECTIVES

The students will:

1. Analyze the role and importance of banks in communities.

2. Explain that savers earn interest from banks for money deposited, and borrowers pay interest to receive money from banks.

TIME REQUIRED

45-60 minutes

MATERIALS

✓ Large blank bulletin board for "the town"

✓ Strips of paper, approximately three to four inches wide, to use as roads in "the town"
  - Before starting the lesson, place the strips of paper (roads) on the bulletin board to make city blocks in the town. Place a picture of a bank in one of the blocks. See diagram below for example.

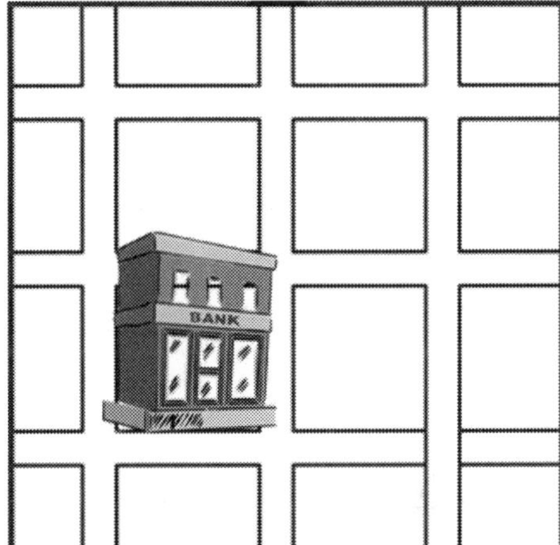

✓ Piece of construction paper with "Community Bank" written on it

✓ One small square of paper for each student, all placed in a paper bag
  - On each square, write either a "1," "2," "3" or "4," so that each number is written on one-fourth of the squares.

✓ Enough three-by-five inch index cards for the following distribution:
  - One fourth of the students will receive one card each; one fourth will receive two cards each; one fourth will receive three cards each; and one fourth will receive four cards each.

✓ Six paper clips for each student

✓ Twenty-five extra paper clips

- ✓ One penny for each student
- ✓ Crayons or markers for decorating houses and businesses
- ✓ Visuals 9.1 and 9.2
- ✓ Scotch tape
- ✓ Bulletin-board tacks
- ✓ A sheet of paper and a marker for each student.
- ✓ One copy of Activity 9.1 for each student

PROCEDURE

1. Ask the students if they have ever gone to a bank with their parents. Ask them why a person might go to a bank. ***To put money in an account or to get a loan***

2. Explain that **income** is the money people receive for the resources they provide in the economy. After taxes are paid, people can either spend or save their income. People can save by putting money in a savings account in a bank. Banks provide a safe place for people to keep their money–safer than keeping it in a house.

3. Explain that **interest** is the price people pay for using other people's money. When people save money in a bank, they earn interest. The interest that a bank pays becomes income to the people who keep their money in the bank.

4. Explain that when people borrow money from a bank, they must pay back what they borrowed, and they must also pay interest on the money they borrowed.

5. Explain that banks are very important for a community.
   - Banks use some of the money that people deposit to make loans. When people or businesses need more money than they have available to spend for things like houses or cars, they borrow money from the bank.
   - Banks make loans to people who would like to start businesses in the community. They also make loans to businesses when the businesses need to buy more products to sell or when businesses need to buy new equipment or machinery.
   - Banks make it easier to transfer money from people who save to people who wish to borrow.

6. Refer the students to the bulletin board. Tell them that they will participate in an activity that will help them understand the role that banks play in a community.

7. Tell the students that some of them will be borrowers, and some of them will be savers, but each student is to build a house or a business for the town.

8. Explain that you will be the banker for this activity. Set up a small desk at the front of the classroom and place a sign reading "Community Bank" on the desk.

9. Distribute six paper clips and one penny to each student. Have each student draw a number from the bag. Distribute one index card to each student who drew a "1," two index cards to each student who drew a "2," three index cards to each student who drew a "3" and four index cards to each student who drew a "4."

10. Explain that the cards and paper clips represent income. Explain that in a community, not all people earn equal amounts of income, so in the classroom, different students received different amounts of income.

11. Tell the students that they will use the index cards to "build" a small house or a large house, or they can start a small business or a large business. They should decorate their houses/businesses and put their names on them.

12. Tell the students that to determine whether they will build a house or a business, and what size their house or business will be, they will flip their pennies and use the instructions in Visual 9.1.

13. Display Visual 9.1. Explain to the students that they are to flip their pennies twice and record whether the penny lands as heads or tails. Display Visual 9.2 and explain the following instructions:

- If the students have the correct number of cards for their individual projects, they can begin building the house or business using their cards.
- The students may tape cards together if their project calls for more than one card.
- Once the students have built a house or business, they may pin or tape it on a street in the bulletin-board town. (Show the students the bulletin-board town.)
- Some of the students may have more cards than they need for their building project. Others may not have as many as they need.
- If the students have more than enough for the project, they may save some of the cards by depositing them in the bank. For each card that a student deposits in the bank, he or she will earn one paper clip in interest.

14. Ask how many students do not have enough cards to build their designated project. Ask those students what they could do to build their business or house. ***Borrow from the bank***

15. Tell the students that to borrow a card from the bank, it will cost them two paper clips in interest. Remind them that one way banks can make a profit is to charge more in interest to those who borrow than it pays to those who save money and deposit their money in the bank.

16. Once each student has saved or borrowed, show the students how the bank's holdings (paper clips) have increased. Also draw the students' attention to how cards were transferred from the savers, to the bank, and then to the borrowers. Leave the town on the bulletin board for further class discussion.

17. Allow time for each student to build a house or business and place it in the town on the bulletin board. Discuss the following questions:

A. What type of business did you start? ***Answers will vary but might include a grocery store, clothing store or restaurant.***

B. What businesses do you think are missing in the community? ***Answers will vary.***

C. In our community, did everyone receive the same income (represented by index cards)? ***No, some students received one, some received two, some received three, and some received four.***

D. Does this represent real life? ***Yes, everyone does not earn the same amount of income in real life.***

E. People use their income to buy goods and services, to save for the future and to pay taxes. How many people in our community used their income to "buy" houses or businesses? ***Answers will vary.*** How many people saved part of their income in the bank? ***Answers will vary.***

F. When people in the community saved at the bank, what did they receive? ***Paper clips***

G. What did the paper clips represent? ***Interest***

H. Why do banks pay interest? ***As a payment for using savers' money***

I. Why did people in the community borrow from the bank? ***To expand businesses, to build new houses, to build new businesses***

J. What did people in the community pay when they borrowed? ***Paper clips***

K. What did the paper clips represent? ***Interest***

L. Why do banks charge interest to people who borrow? ***People who borrow are using someone else's money. Interest is the payment they make for using someone else's money.***

M. If you were to receive more interest (two paper clips) for each card you put in the bank instead of one, how would this affect how much you would be willing to save? ***They would put more cards in the bank if they had extra cards.***

CLOSURE

18. Explain that the students will play a game called "Fact or Fiction" to review the content of the lesson. Divide the students into pairs. Distribute a piece of paper and a marker to each student. Tell the students that they will listen to statements related to the lesson. For each statement, they must decide whether the statement is fact—a true statement–or fiction—a false statement. Have one student in each pair write a "T" for "true" on his or her sheet of paper. Have the other student in each pair write an "F" for "false" on his or her sheet of paper. Once a statement is read, the pairs should decide whether the statement is fact or fiction and hold up the appropriate sheet of paper. Once all the pairs have answered, the students will be asked to correct the fiction statements to make them fact.

A. People can spend or save their after-tax income. ***Fact—true***

B. Many people choose to put the money they save in the fireplace. ***Fiction—false; correction—bank***

C. People choose to put their savings in a bank because it is safer than keeping it other places and because banks pay interest. ***Fact—true***

D. Banks make it harder to transfer money from savers to borrowers. ***Fiction-false; correction—easier***

E. If I borrow money from the bank, I must pay the bank what I owe plus more money called a "vault." ***Fiction—false; correction—interest***

F. People borrow from a bank because they don't have all the money they need to buy or build something. ***Fact—true***

G. If I want to expand my business, I will go to the bank to open a savings account. ***Fiction—false; correction—to get a loan***

H. Banks charge borrowers more interest than they pay to savers. ***Fact—true***

I. If banks decided not to make loans, there would be fewer houses and businesses in the town. ***Fact—true***

J. If everyone who saved part of their income decided not to put it in the bank, but instead put it under their mattresses, the bank wouldn't have money to make loans. ***Fact—true***

ASSESSMENT

Distribute a copy of Activity 9.1 to each student. Allow time for the students to complete the work. Review their answers.

Answers:

1. Billy got a job delivering newspapers. Each week he earned $20. He put half of his money in his ***savings account*** at the ***bank*** downtown. The ***bank*** paid Billy ***interest.***

2. Mrs. Franklin wanted to build a ***house***, but she didn't have enough money to pay the entire cost of building the ***house.*** She decided to ***borrow*** money from the bank downtown. The bank gave Mrs. Franklin a ***loan*** for her ***house.*** Mrs. Franklin agreed to pay the bank later, plus pay ***interest*** on each dollar that the bank let her ***borrow.***

3. Part of Billy's ***savings*** was used to make part of Mrs. Franklin's ***loan.*** By ***saving*** money for his new bike in the downtown bank, Billy helped Mrs. Franklin build her new ***house.***

Visual 9.1 - **Bulletin-Board Banking**

PENNY TOSS OUTCOMES

If the first toss is "heads" and the second toss is "heads," you want to start a large business. You will need four cards.

If the first toss is "heads" and the second toss is "tails," you want to build a large house. You will need three cards.

If the first toss is "tails" and the second toss is "heads," you want to start a small business. You will need two cards.

If the first toss is "tails" and the second toss is "tails," you want to build a small house. You will need one card.

Visual 9.2 - **Building, Borrowing and Saving**

✓ If you have the correct number of cards for your individual project, you may begin building the house or business using your cards.

✓ You may tape cards together if your project calls for more than one card.

✓ Once you have built a house or business, you may pin or tape it on a street in the bulletin-board town.

✓ Some of you may have more cards than you need for your building project. Others may not have as many as you need.

✓ If you have more than enough for the project, you may save some of the cards by depositing them in the bank. For each card that you deposit in the bank, you will earn one paper clip in interest.

Activity 9.1 - **Assessment**

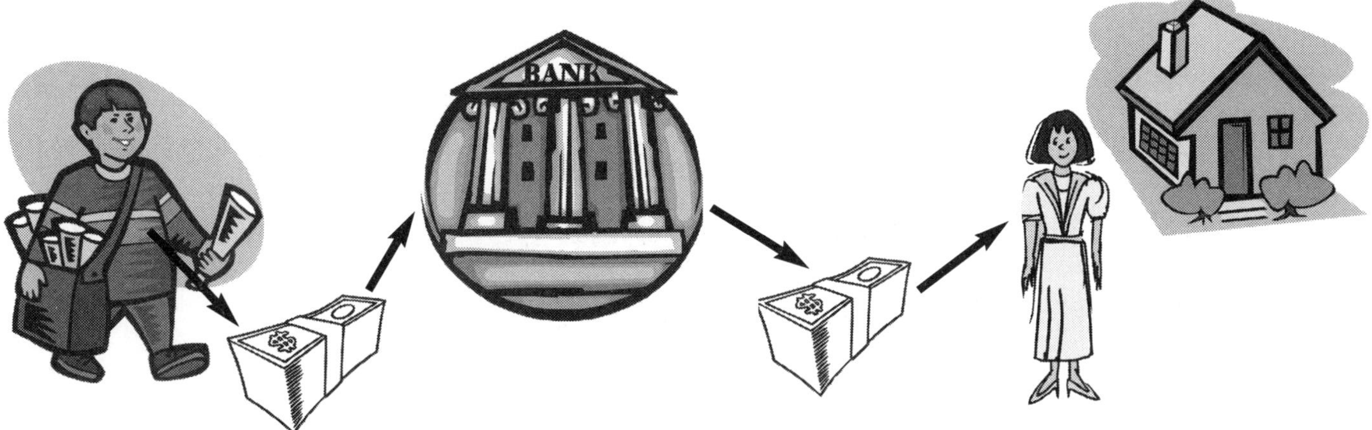

Write a story by filling in the blanks in the sentences below. Use the word bank below and the information you have learned in class to help you. You may use the words in the word bank more than once.

Saving	Interest	Loan	Borrow	Savings Account
	Savings	House	Bank	

1. Billy got a job delivering newspapers. Each week he earned $20. He put half of his money in his _______________ at the _______________downtown. The _______________ paid Billy _______________.

2. Mrs. Franklin wanted to build a _______________, but she didn't have enough money to pay the entire cost of building the _______________. She decided to _______________ money from the bank downtown. The bank gave Mrs. Franklin a _______________ for her _______________. Mrs. Franklin agreed to pay the bank later, plus pay _______________ on each dollar that the bank let her _______________.

3. Part of Billy's _______________ was used to make part of Mrs. Franklin's _______________. By _______________ money for his new bike in the downtown bank, Billy helped Mrs. Franklin build her new _______________.

Lesson 10 - **What Makes Money Acceptable**

LESSON DESCRIPTION

In this lesson, the students participate in a demonstration to identify the characteristics that make something a good form of money. Following the demonstration, the students learn about changes that were made to U.S. currency to protect the integrity of the currency by reducing the possibility of counterfeiting. For additional information about U.S. currency, teachers may want to visit www.moneyfactory.com, the Web site of the Bureau of Engraving and Printing. The NCEE is grateful to the Bureau of Engraving and Printing for its assistance with this lesson.

CONCEPTS

Characteristics of money
Money

CONTENT STANDARD

Standard 11 – Role of Money

- **Benchmark 1 for 4th grade:** Money is anything widely accepted as final payment for goods and services.

OBJECTIVES

The students will:

1. Define money.
2. Identify the characteristics of money.
3. Identify security features that protect the integrity of U.S. currency.

TIME REQUIRED

90-120 minutes

MATERIALS

✓ U.S. dollar and U.S. coins
✓ Items for classroom demonstration:
- Handful of salt
- A children's paperback book with chapters
- Empty bowl
- Glass or cup of water
- Very heavy item, such as a rock or bowling ball
- One piece of brown construction paper with the word "beef" written on it
- One empty jar with a lid

✂ One pair of scissors for each student
✓ Visuals 10.1 and 10.2
✓ One highlighting marker for each pair of students
✓ One copy of Activities 10.1 and 10.5 for each student
✓ One copy of Activity 10.2 for each student (**NOTE:** To follow government regulations, do not enlarge or reduce the copy of the currency.)
✓ One copy of Activities 10.3 and 10.4 for each pair of students
✓ (Optional) New $50 note and one magnifying glass

PROCEDURE

Day 1

1. Introduce the lesson by showing the students a $1 bill and some coins. Ask the students why people want money. ***To buy goods and services, to save to buy goods and services in the future***

2. Explain that today most societies use some form of coins and paper bills, or currency, as money. However, throughout history, other things have been used as money, such as shells, gold, silver, chickens, tobacco and fur.

Define **money** as anything widely used as final payment for goods and services. Money is a way, or medium, for making trades or exchanges. Ask the students what characteristics would make something useful as a medium of exchange. ***Accept students' ideas.***

3. Choose five students. Give one student a handful of salt, one student a book, one student a heavy item such as a rock, another student a piece of brown construction paper labeled "beef" and another student an empty, sealed jar. Read the following scenarios.

- Have the student with the salt show the handful of salt to the class.

Scenario 1: James is on his way to school. He has a handful of salt. His school accepts salt as payment for lunch at school. On the way to school it begins to rain very hard. James gets soaked.

Pause and have the student with the handful of salt come up to the desk. Tell the student to place his or her hand over the bowl on the desk. Pour water over the salt. Ask the students why James' salt is not tradable any more. ***It dissolved.*** Ask the students if this makes trade easier or more difficult. ***More difficult*** Why? ***Salt isn't durable, it dissolves.***

- Have the student with the book show the book to the class.

Scenario 2: Susan wants a pack of gum. Susan's friend is willing to trade with her. Susan has a book to trade, but she thinks the book is more valuable than one pack of gum.

Pause and ask the class what would happen if Susan tore the first few pages, the last few pages, or a few middle pages out of the book and gave it to her friend in exchange for the gum. ***Her friend wouldn't be able to enjoy reading the book because he or she wouldn't know how the story began or how it ended.*** Ask the students if this makes trade easier or more difficult. ***More difficult*** Why? ***It is hard to trade if the item used isn't divisible, because all items aren't equal in value.***

- Have the student with the rock (or other heavy item) show the rock to the class.

Scenario 3: Rico's country uses rocks (or some other heavy item) as money. Rico has to carry heavy rocks with him whenever he wants to make a purchase.

Pause and have the student with the heavy item walk back and forth in front of the room. Ask the student how he or she would feel about carrying this item all of the time in order to buy things. ***Tired, wouldn't like it*** Ask the class if this makes trade easier or more difficult. ***More difficult*** Why? ***It is difficult to trade when you must carry very heavy things around with you.***

- Have the student holding the "beef" sign show the sign to the class.

Scenario 4: Ta-Keesha raises cattle. She takes some of the beef from her cattle to exchange for other goods and services that she wants. Ta-Keesha takes some beef to the baker to buy some bread. The baker is a vegetarian and won't accept beef or any other meat as payment.

Pause and ask the student with the beef sign how he or she feels about this problem. ***Unhappy, frustrated*** Ask the class if there might be other people unwilling to accept beef as payment for things. ***Yes*** Ask the class if this makes trade easier or more difficult. ***More difficult*** Why? ***It is hard to trade if people won't accept the item you have to trade.***

- Have the student holding the jar of air show the jar to the class.

Scenario 5: Curt has a jar of air. Everyone breathes air, so Curt has decided to trade the jar of air for other things that he wants. But no one will trade with Curt.

Pause and ask the student holding the jar of air how he or she feels about this problem. ***Unhappy, frustrated*** Ask the class why no one wants to trade with the student. ***Everyone has air.*** Ask the students if trading with a good that everyone has makes trade easier or more difficult. ***More difficult*** Why? ***If everyone has***

their own or can get their own, they aren't willing to trade.

4. Tell the students who participated in the demonstration to return to their seats. Display Visual 10.1. Explain that if an item is a good form of money, it will be useful as a medium of exchange. A good medium of exchange will have all five of the characteristics listed on Visual 10.1. Ask the students to listen to an explanation of each characteristic and to think about the demonstration that just took place in class. Explain each characteristic as follows.

   • **Portable** means easy to carry. If people want to use something as a form of money, they want it to be portable so that trading will be easier. This means that an item used as money should be easy to carry with you to make exchanges. Ask the students which item(s) in the demonstration was difficult to carry. ***The heavy item, salt, beef*** Tell the students that long ago, people used rocks, shells, gold and even cows as forms of money. However, it was not easy to carry enough rocks or cows to make a large purchase. Ask the students where and how they carry their money. ***Pocket, wallet, purse***

   • **Durable** means that an item is long-lasting. It can withstand being folded, carried in pockets or wallets or even washed. People want money that won't dissolve, rot or crumble. Ask the students which item(s) in the demonstration was not very durable. ***Salt, beef*** Explain that salt was not very durable because it dissolved. Beef would not be very durable either because it would spoil.

   • **Divisible** means that an item is easy to divide into larger or smaller amounts. If something is divisible, it is easy to have the right amount to exchange for other items. In the demonstration, which item lost its value when it was divided? ***The book*** Point out that the heavy item would not be easy to divide, nor would a cow. Most societies have different denominations of coins and currency so that people can more easily pay for items they want. Explain that having different denominations of U.S. coins and currency provides divisibility. Ask the students what the denominations of coins and currency are in the U.S. ***Penny, nickel, dime, quarter, $1 coin, $1 bill, $5 bill, $10 bill, $20 bill, $50 bill, $100 bill***

   • **Generally acceptable** means that most people are willing to accept a form of money as payment for other goods and services. In the demonstration, which item wasn't generally acceptable? ***Beef*** Point out that in our society, salt, books, air and rocks are not generally acceptable either. Ask the students what would happen if they tried to buy lunch in the school cafeteria with gum. ***The people in the cafeteria wouldn't accept it. Gum is not generally acceptable for exchange in our society.*** Money that is **uniform** is more readily acceptable. This means that most people expect the quality of one piece of currency, one coin or one item serving as money to be the same as another piece of currency, another coin or another item serving as money. In the demonstration, which items might not be uniform? ***Salt, beef, book, rock, air*** Point out that in our society the quality of these items might vary, and this would make the items less acceptable to people.

   • **Relatively scarce** means that an item used as money must not be freely available. Everyone shouldn't be able to draw, grow or find it. In the demonstration, which item wasn't relatively scarce? ***The jar filled with air*** If everyone can make or find an item easily, no one would want to accept it for other goods because they would be able to make or find the item themselves. If many people could raise their own cattle like the student in the earlier demonstration, beef wouldn't be relatively scarce. Rocks and shells are not generally scarce; societies that used rocks or shells for money actually used specific types of rocks and shells that were more difficult to find.

5. Remind the students that most items used as money that have these five important characteristics would be a good medium of exchange. Distribute a copy of Activity 10.1 to each student. Show the students the $1 bill

and coins again and ask the following questions. Tell the students to write notes on Activity 10.1 as needed.

A. Is our currency portable? ***It is lightweight. It is small. It is easy to carry. It can be folded up and stuffed in a sock.***

B. Are U.S. currency notes durable? ***Yes*** Point out that the average life of a $1 bill is 18 months. The life of higher denomination notes is longer. Remind students that U.S. currency survives the washer and the dryer when left in a pants pocket.

C. Is the $1 bill divisible? ***No*** How do our bills and coins give us divisibility? ***They come in different denominations–$1, $5, $10, $20 and penny, nickel, dime, quarter. This means that we can make change and pay the amount we think an item is worth.***

D. Are U.S. dollars generally acceptable? ***Yes*** Point out that people accept U.S. dollars as payment for their work and in exchange for goods, services and resources. Is U.S. currency uniform in quality? ***Yes, it is carefully designed to be uniform.***

E. Is U.S. money relatively scarce? ***Students will likely answer yes because they have heard their parents say there is not enough money.*** Point out that the Federal Reserve System controls the amount of money available in the U.S. economy.

6. Review the important content of the lesson by asking the following questions:

A. What do people use to buy the things that they want? ***Money***

B. What characteristics make something useful as money—what makes money a good medium of exchange? ***Useful money is money that is portable, durable, divisible, generally acceptable and relatively scarce.***

Day 2

7. Distribute a copy of Activity 10.2 and a pair of scissors to each student. Explain that this is a reduced copy of a $20 United States note. Instruct the students to cut the note out along the dotted lines and to fold it on the solid line. Ask the students if they think it is possible to use the copy to buy lunch in the school cafeteria. ***No*** Why not? ***It isn't real money.*** Discuss the following questions:

A. How can you and other people tell whether the currency they receive is real or genuine? ***Answers will vary. It is unlikely that the students will have any idea how they can tell whether a note is genuine.***

B. What would happen if the people working at a local store accepted money that wasn't genuine? ***Answers will vary.***

8. Explain that if people accept money that isn't genuine, they are "stuck" with that money. People at other stores, people at banks, and so on, might recognize that the money is not real and would not accept it as payment for other goods and services. Explain that if this happened often, many people would lose faith in the value of money. They would not be willing to accept it, which would make exchange more difficult.

9. Tell the students that it is very important for people to trust that the money they use is genuine, or real. Thus government has laws that make it illegal to produce counterfeit money. Explain that counterfeit means something that has been made to look real, but isn't. Collect the copies of the $20 bill from the students.

10. Point out that not only is there a law against making counterfeit or fake money, but the government also designs money to make it difficult for someone to produce counterfeit or fake money. The government changes currency to make it more difficult to counterfeit. For example, on September 28, 2004, the government introduced a new $50 note that has many features designed to make counterfeiting more difficult.

11. Divide the students into pairs. Distribute highlighting markers and a copy of Activities 10.3 and 10.4 to each pair of students.

12. Display Visual 10.2. Explain that the visual is a picture of the front and back of the new U.S. $50 note that went into circulation on September 28, 2004. Explain that each pair of students has an picture of the front and back of the new $50 note. Point out the important security features that are part of the bill. Tell the students to use the highlighting marker and take notes to remind them of these features. (**NOTE:** If possible, have a new $50 note available to show the color and to demonstrate the watermark and color-shifting ink.)

• **Watermark:** The watermark is part of the paper itself and can be seen from both sides of the bill.

• **Security thread:** A security thread, or plastic strip, is embedded in the paper and runs vertically to the right of the portrait. If you look very closely, you will see that the words "USA 50" and a small flag are visible along the thread from both sides of the bill.

• **Color-shifting ink:** While looking at an actual $50 bill, tilt the bill up and down. You will notice that the number "50" in the lower right corner changes color from copper to green.

• **Microprinting:** There are four different words, numbers or phrases microprinted onto the new $50 bill. Microprinting means these words, numbers or phrases are so small that they are difficult to see, and very difficult to counterfeit. Look for FIFTY, USA, 50, and THE UNITED STATES OF AMERICA on the bill.

• **Federal Reserve indicators** and **serial numbers:** A seal representing the Federal Reserve System and a letter with serial numbers are on every bill. Every bill has a unique combination of 11 numbers and letters that appear twice on the front of the bill.

• **Symbols of freedom:** There are new symbols on the $50 note that represent the American flag. Stars and stripes are printed in blue and red behind the portrait of Ulysses S. Grant. A field of blue stars is located to the left of Grant's portrait. Three red stripes are located to the right of the portrait. A small, metallic silver-blue star is located to the right of the portrait.

• **Color:** Subtle red and blue background colors have been added to both sides of the note. Small yellow "50s" have been printed in the background on the back of the note.

• **Updated portrait and vignette:** There no longer is a border surrounding the portrait of Grant on the front of the note or the U.S. Capitol on the back of the note. The portrait has been moved up, and the shoulders have been extended. (**NOTE:** The picture on the back of the bill is called a vignette.)

13. Remind the students that the government provides these features to make sure that everyone can trust that U.S. currency will be accepted in exchange for goods, services and resources.

CLOSURE

14. Review the important points of the lesson by asking the following questions:

A. What are the characteristics that make something useful as money? ***To be useful, money should be portable, durable, divisible, generally acceptable and relatively scarce.***

B. Why is U.S. currency portable? ***It is easy to carry. It folds easily to put in a wallet or pocket.***

C. Is U.S. currency durable? ***Yes*** How do you know? ***It survives the washer and dryer.*** Remind students that a $1 bill lasts about 18 months.

D. How do you know that U.S. currency is divisible? ***There are different denominations of coins and currency.***

E. How do you know that U.S. currency is generally acceptable? ***People accept U.S. currency as payment for work. Stores accept it as payment for goods and services.***

F. What does "counterfeit" mean? ***Fake***

G. How does the U.S. government protect against counterfeit currency? ***By making bills that are more difficult for people to copy.***

H. What makes U.S. currency scarce? ***It is hard to obtain; the Federal Reserve controls the amount of currency in circulation; the federal government makes it illegal to counterfeit money; the U.S. government makes currency so that it is hard to copy***

ASSESSMENT

Distribute a copy of Activity 10.5 to each student. Allow time for the students to answer the questions.

Answers:

1. Circle one of the following items. ***Answers will vary.***

2. Explain whether the item you circled has each of the qualities that make money a good medium of exchange. ***The students should explain how well the item meets the five characteristics of money.***

- ***Bar of gold:***
  - ✦ ***Durable–doesn't break or chip easily***
  - ✦ ***Not portable–heavy and not easy to carry***
  - ✦ ***Not divisible–not easy to divide, would require special tools to cut***
  - ✦ ***Generally acceptable–Most people would be willing to accept gold in exchange for other things; there might be variations in the quality and weight of the gold.***
  - ✦ ***Relatively scarce–not many people have access to gold.***

- ***Jug of water:***
  - ✦ ***Not durable–could easily break or spill***
  - ✦ ***Not portable—not easy to carry around***
  - ✦ ***Divisible–water could be divided by fractions of cups***
  - ✦ ***Not generally acceptable–Most people would not accept water in exchange for other things; the quality of the water may not be uniform.***
  - ✦ ***Not relatively scarce–most people have easy access to water.***

- ***Pack of chewing gum:***
  - ✦ ***Not durable–breaks, dries up, can't be reused once chewed***
  - ✦ ***Portable–is small and easy to carry around in a pocket, purse or wallet***
  - ✦ ***Divisible–could trade one piece or even several pieces, as opposed to entire pack***
  - ✦ ***Not generally acceptable–Most people would not accept gum in exchange for other goods and services; the quality and size of the packs of gum would vary.***
  - ✦ ***Not relatively scarce–people have easy access to gum, people could make their own gum.***

3. Describe three of the security features on the new $50 bill. ***The students should explain any of the features discussed, including watermark, security thread, color-shifting ink, microprinting, Federal Reserve indicators, serial numbers, symbols of freedom, color, updated portrait and vignette.***

Visual 10.1 - **Money**

Money: A Medium of Exchange

* People exchange money for goods and services.

Five desirable characteristics for something to be useful as money:

1. Portable

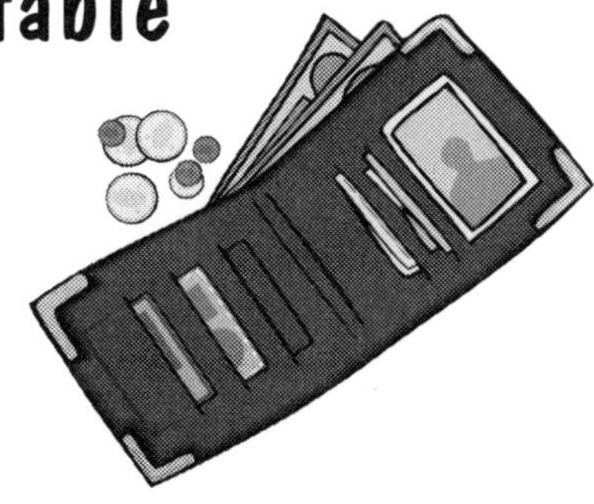

2. Durable

3. Divisible

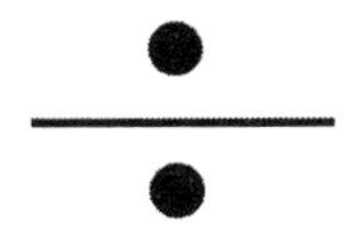

4. Generally Acceptable

5. Relatively Scarce

Visual 10.2 - **Money Security**

Activity 10.1 - **Characteristics of Money**

Money: A Medium of Exchange
U.S. Dollars and Coins

1. Portable

2. Durable

3. Divisible

4. Generally Acceptable

5. Relatively Scarce

Activity 10.2 - **Twenty-Dollar Bill**

Cut the bill out along the dotted line. Fold the two parts along the solid line.

Activity 10.3 - **Fifty-Dollar Note–Front**

Activity 10.4 - **Fifty Dollar Note–Back**

Activity 10.5 - **Assessment**

1. Circle one of the following items.

Bars of Gold

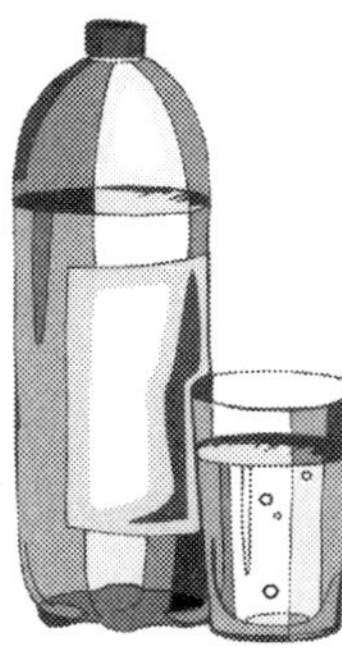

Water

Gum

2. Explain whether the item you circled has each of the qualities that make money a good medium of exchange.

Portable ______________________________

____

Durable ______________________________

____

Divisible ______________________________

____

Acceptable ______________________________

____

Relatively Scarce ______________________________

____

Activity 10.5 - (continued) **Assessment**

3. Describe three of the security features found on the new $50 bill.

a. ____

____

____

____

b. ____

____

____

____

c. ____

____

____

____

Lesson 11 - **How Many Snacks Will the Students Buy?**

LESSON DESCRIPTION

In this lesson, the students role-play as consumers with a fixed amount to spend. They react to changes in price for a favorite snack food. The students use the data from this activity to describe the relationship between price and quantity demanded. They consider other examples and learn that the price-quantity relationship holds for most goods. They learn that this relationship is called the law of demand.

CONCEPTS

Consumers
Law of demand
Price

CONTENT STANDARDS

Standard 7 – Markets — Price and Quantity Determination

- **Benchmark 1 for 4th grade:** A price is what people pay when they buy a good or service, and what they receive when they sell a good or service.

Standard 8 – Markets — Role of Price in the Market System

- **Benchmark 1 for 4th grade:** Higher prices for a good or service provide incentives for buyers to purchase less of that good or service and for producers to make or sell more of it. Lower prices for a good or service provide incentives for buyers to purchase more of that good or service and for producers to make or sell less of it.
- **Benchmark 1 for 8th grade:** An increase in the price of a good or service encourages people to look for substitutes, causing the quantity demanded to decrease, and vice versa. This relationship between price and quantity demanded, known as the law of demand, exists as long as other factors influencing demand do not change.

OBJECTIVES

The students will:

1. Define price and consumers.
2. Describe the relationship between price and the amounts people are willing and able to buy.
3. Define the law of demand.
4. Analyze why the inverse relationship between price and the amounts people will buy exists.

TIME REQUIRED

45-60 minutes

MATERIALS

✓ Copies of fliers from grocery stores, discount stores and department stores
✓ (Optional) Four pieces of construction paper with snack names written on them (*Examples: potato chips, corn chips, granola bars, candy bars)*
✓ (Optional) Masking tape
✓ One sheet of paper for each student
✓ Visuals 11.1 and 11.2
✓ One copy of Activities 11.1, 11.2 and 11.3 for each student
✓ (Optional) Snacks for the students

PROCEDURE

1. Show the students fliers from grocery stores, discount stores and department stores. Point out that these are sale fliers and that stores distribute these types of fliers to consumers all the time. **Consumers** are people who buy and use

goods and services. When consumers look at the fliers, they see that the prices for goods and services have been reduced. Explain that **price** is the amount people pay when they buy a good or service and the amount sellers receive when they sell a good or service. Ask the students why they think stores put items on sale—that is, reduce the price for items. ***Answers will vary, but might include: people buy more, more people come to the store.***

2. Tell the students that they will role-play as buyers to see how buyers react to changes in the price of a good or service.

3. Write the names of four types of snacks along the top of the chalkboard, or tape four signs, each with one snack name written on it, along the top of the chalkboard–e.g., fruit snacks, corn chips, granola bar, candy bar.

4. Explain that each student has a budget of $4.00 to spend and may buy one type of snack. Each snack weighs two ounces, and the price for each snack is $1.00. Discuss the following:

    A. How many of a particular snack are you able to buy with $4.00? ***Four***

    B. What else will influence how many you buy? ***How hungry I am, if the snacks are healthy or not, how much I like a particular snack, how much other snacks cost***

5. Tell the students they may spend their four dollars in any way they like. Distribute one sheet of paper to each student and have the students write down their choices. For example, a student might list a fruit snack, a package of corn chips and two candy bars. Select one of the snacks and have the students hold up fingers to represent how many of that snack they would buy. Under the appropriate sign on the chalkboard, record the total quantity of that snack that the class would buy. Continue this process with the remaining three types of snacks.

6. Select the snack for which the students have indicated they would buy the largest quantity. Display Visual 11.1. Fill in the name of the most popular snack in the title of the table. In the column titled "Number of Packages the Students Are Willing and Able to Buy," across from a price of $1.00, record the number of packages of that snack the students would be willing and able to buy.

7. Announce that the price of the other snacks is still $1.00, but that the price of the most popular snack is now $2.00. Remind the students that each of them still has $4.00 to spend. Ask if any students want to change their minds about what snacks to purchase. Have the students indicate how many of the most popular snack they are now willing and able to buy.

8. Record the new quantity for the most popular snack on Visual 11.1 in the "Number of Packages the Students Are Willing and Able to Buy" column, across from a price of $2.00.

9. Repeat steps 7 and 8, for the most popular snack, for prices of $3.00 and $4.00.

10. Distribute a copy of Activity 11.1 to each student and tell the students to fill in the blank in the title of the table with the name of the most popular snack, and to transfer the data from Visual 11.1 to the table on Activity 11.1. (**NOTE:** The price of the other snacks remained at $1.00 throughout this activity.)

11. Discuss the following:

    A. What happened to the number of packages you bought when the price rose from $1.00 to $2.00? ***The number of packages decreased.***

    B. What happened to the number of packages you bought when the price rose from $2.00 to $3.00? ***The number of packages decreased.***

    C. What happened to the number of packages you bought when the price rose from $3.00 to $4.00? ***The number of packages decreased.***

D. What would happen to the number of packages you would buy if the price decreased from $4.00 to $3.00? ***The number of packages would increase.***

E. What can we conclude about the students' snack-buying behavior and the price of snacks? ***As the price of snacks goes up, the amount the students want to buy goes down. As the price of snacks goes down, the amount the students want to buy goes up.***

12. Tell the students to answer the questions on Activity 11.1. Review the students' answers by discussing the following:

A. Why did you buy fewer packages of the snack as the price increased? ***With only $4.00 to spend, the students weren't able to buy as many packages as the price increased. As the price increased, the students were willing to substitute a less expensive snack for the more expensive snack.***

B. What snacks did you buy instead? ***Answers will vary.*** Why? ***Those snacks cost less and I like them almost as well.***

13. Explain that the data collected for the preferred snack can also be shown on a graph. Display a transparency of Visual 11.2, and distribute a copy of Activity 11.2 to each student.

14. Complete the title of the graph in Visual 11.2 by writing the name of the most popular snack in the blank space on the transparency. Have the students do the same on their activity sheet. Label the vertical axis "Price" and the horizontal axis "Quantity," and have the students do the same.

15. As a class, scale each axis:

- Along the vertical axis, make marks to indicate the different prices that might be paid for the snack, with $1.00 the lowest mark, and higher prices at each higher mark.
- Along the horizontal axis, make marks to indicate the amount of candy bars the students indicated they would buy when discussing different prices. For example, the first mark might be 2, the second mark might be 4, and so on, according to the results of the class surveys.

16. Plot the points on the graph with the data contained in Activity 11.1. Connect the points on the transparency, and have the students do the same. Discuss the following:

A. What does the graph/curve look like? ***Like a slide—it slopes down from the vertical axis to the right***

B. Why does the graph/curve look like this? ***Because as the price of the snack increases, people are willing and able to buy fewer packages, and as the price of the snack decreases, people are willing and able to buy more packages***

17. Tell the students that they should imagine what might happen in each of the following situations. Discuss the following:

A. How would consumer behavior change if water that used to sell for a price of $2.00 a cup now sold for a price of $20 a cup? ***People wouldn't bathe as often, people wouldn't wash their cars or water their lawns, people wouldn't drink as much water.***

B. If water sold for a price of $20 a cup, would consumers buy more or less water? ***Less***

C. How would consumer behavior change if ice cream that used to sell for $1.75 a scoop now sold for a price of $.01 per scoop? ***People would eat ice cream at every meal, people would feed their pets ice cream.***

D. If ice cream sold for a price of $.01 per scoop, would consumers buy more or less ice cream? ***More***

E. How would consumer behavior change if pencils that used to sell for a price of $1 each now sold for a price of $10 each? ***People wouldn't use pencils for tests, people would write with pens, people would only write using the computer.***

F. If pencils sold for a price of $10 each, would consumers buy more or fewer pencils? ***Fewer***

G. How would consumer behavior change if gold that used to sell for a price of $425 an ounce, now sold for a price of $1 per ounce?

Houses would be made of gold, dishes would be made of gold, cars would be made of gold.

H. If gold sold for a price of $1 per ounce, would consumers buy more or less gold? ***More***

18. Point out that when prices rise, people can't buy as much with the same amount of income as they could before the price went up. Also, when prices rise, people will substitute less expensive products for more expensive products. Refer to the advertising fliers and give examples such as the following:

- If oranges are on sale, people will buy more oranges instead of buying more expensive fruit such as strawberries or apples.
- If one brand of cola is on sale, people will buy more of that cola instead of a more expensive cola.
- If a person has $20 to buy cupcakes for a school party and the price of cupcakes is $1.00, the person can buy 20 cupcakes. If the price of cupcakes is $.50, the person can buy 40 cupcakes.

19. Explain that the idea that people buy more of something at lower prices and less of something at higher prices is so common and happens so often that economists actually call this idea a law—the **law of demand.** The law of demand states that when the price of a product increases, consumers will buy less of it, and when the price of a product decreases, consumers will buy more of it. Have the students write the definition of the law of demand on the back of Activity 11.2.

20. Display Visual 11.2 with the graph. Point out that the downward shape of the line on their graph shows the law of demand. Because consumers have a limited amount to spend, they are willing and able to buy less as price goes up, and they are willing and able to buy more as price goes down.

21. (Optional) Give each student a snack.

CLOSURE

22. Review the important content of the lesson by asking the following questions:

A. What is a price? ***The amount people pay when they buy a good or service and the amount sellers receive when they sell a good or service***

B. What price do you pay for a soda or snack from a vending machine? ***Answers will vary.***

C. What are consumers? ***People who buy and use goods and services***

D. If the price of milk decreases, what will happen to the quantity of milk consumers are willing and able to buy? ***It will increase.***

E. What is the law of demand? ***When the price of a product increases, consumers will buy less of it, and when the price of a product decreases, consumers will buy more of it.***

F. Why is the law of demand true for most products? ***Because consumers with a limited amount to spend aren't able to buy as much as price goes up, and are able to buy more as price goes down; because when price goes up, consumers will buy less of the more expensive product and substitute a less expensive product.***

G. If we graph the prices and the amounts people will buy at those prices, what will the graph look like? ***It will slope downward, a slide, it will start up high near the vertical axis and slope down to the right.***

ASSESSMENT

Distribute a copy of Activity 11.3 to each student. Allow time for the students to complete their work. Review their answers.

Answers:

1. The price for chocolate candy bars was $1.00 each, but now the price is $.75 each. Write a sentence telling what you would expect buyers to do and explain why. ***Buyers will buy more candy bars because each candy bar costs less, because consumers with a limited amount to spend aren't able to buy as much as price***

goes up, and are able to buy more as price goes down.

2. The price of hot dogs at the ballpark was $1.50 each, but now the price is $3.00 each. Write a sentence telling what you would expect buyers to do and explain why. ***Buyers will buy fewer hot dogs because each hot dog costs more. Because consumers have a limited amount to spend, they are able to buy less as price goes up and buy more as price goes down.***

3. If your allowance is $1.75 a week, and the price of video games is $.25 per game, how many video games could you play in a week? ***Seven video games***

4. If your allowance is $1.75 a week and the price of video games increased to $.50 per game, how many video games could you play in a week? ***Three video games***

5. When the price of video games increased in question #4, were you able to play more or fewer video games in a week? Why? ***Fewer. Because I only had $1.75 when the price increased, I was not able to play as many games.***

6. Circle "more" or "less" to make the following statement true. ***The students should circle "less" in the first instance and "more" in the second instance.***

Visual 11.1 - **How Many Are the Students Willing and Able to Buy?**

Table 1: Prices and the Number of Packages of ________________ the Students Are Willing and Able to Buy

Price	Number of Packages the Students Are Willing and Able to Buy
$1.00	
$2.00	
$3.00	
$4.00	

Visual 11.2 - **Graphing Price and Quantity the Students Are Willing and Able to Buy**

Use the price and quantity data recorded on Activity 11.1 from the class demonstration to create a line graph.

Graph of Prices and Quantities of ________________ Students Are Willing and Able to Buy

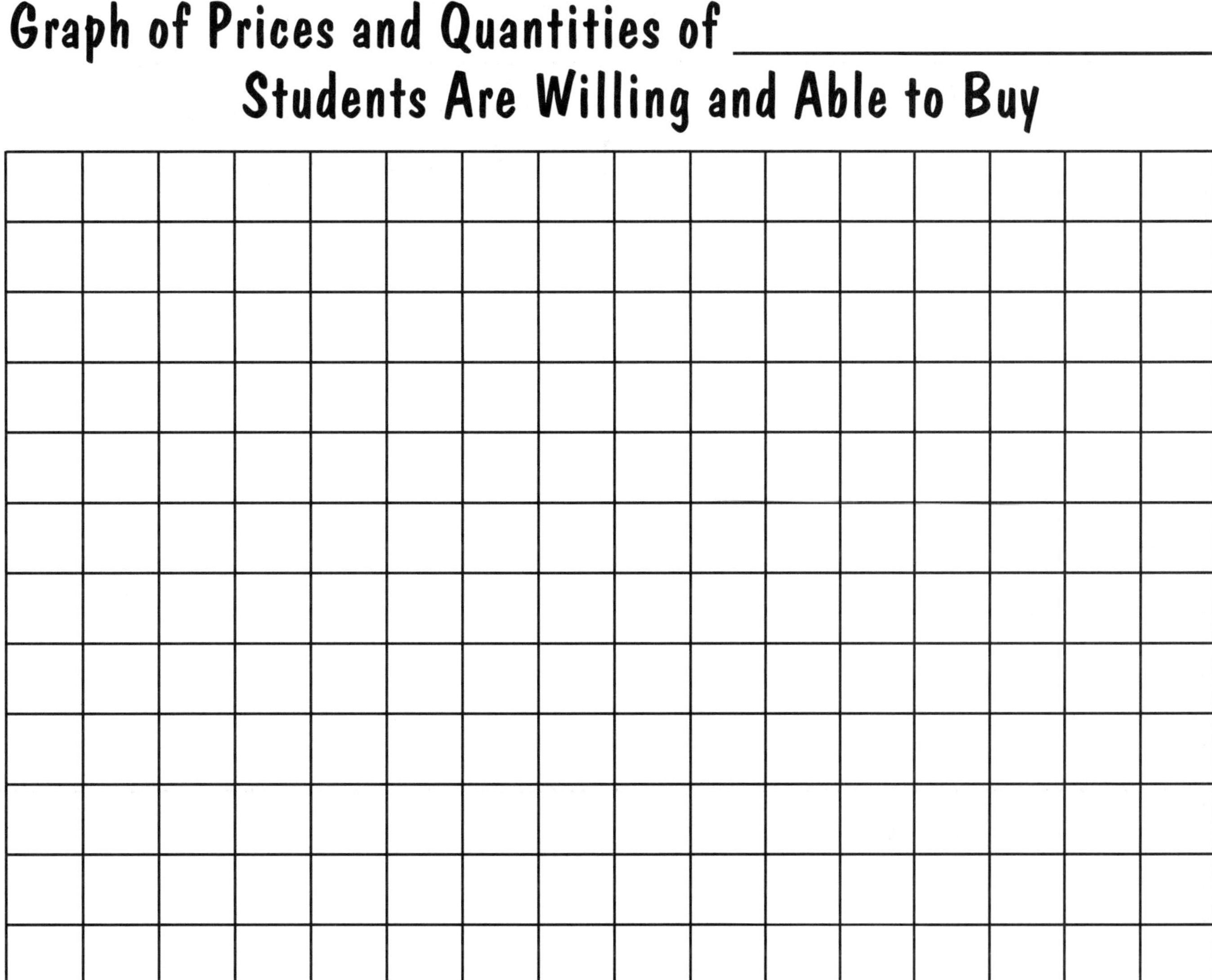

Activity 11.1 - **How Many Will the Students Buy?**

Table 1: Prices and the Number of Packages of ____________ the Students Are Willing and Able to Buy

Price	Number of Packages the Students Are Willing and Able to Buy
$1.00	
$2.00	
$3.00	
$4.00	

Write a sentence to answer questions 1 and 2.

1. If you changed your choice, explain why. ________________________________

____

____

2. If you bought less of this snack, what snack would you buy instead? Why?________________________________

____

____

Activity 11.2 - **Graphing Prices and Quantities**

Use the price and quantity data recorded on Activity 11.1 from the class demonstration to create a line graph.

Graph of Prices and Quantities of ____________ the Students Are Willing and Able to Buy

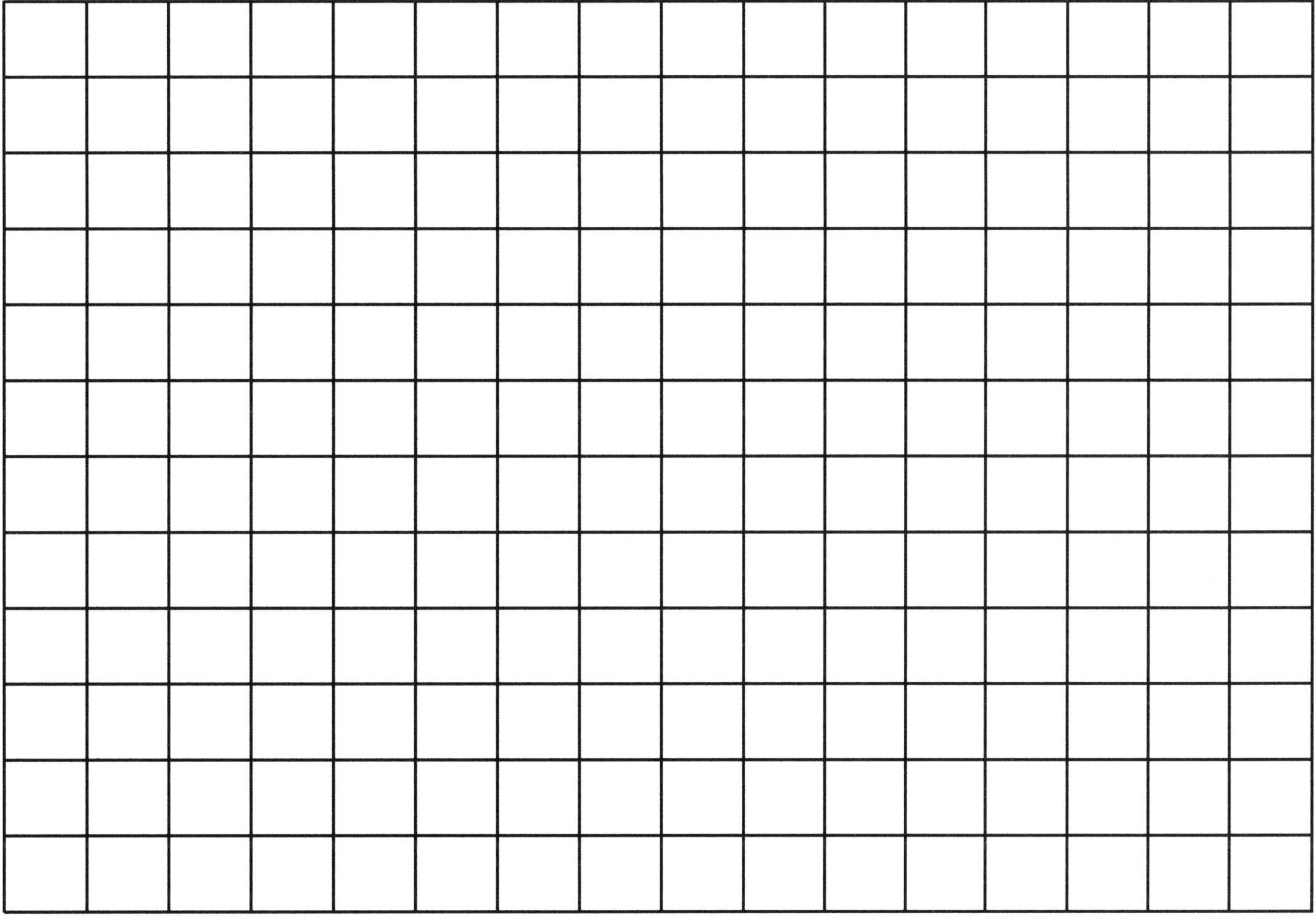

Activity 11.3 - **Assessment**

1. The price for chocolate candy bars was $1.00 each, but now the price is $ .75 each. Write a sentence telling what you would expect buyers to do and explain why.

2. The price of hot dogs at the ballpark was $1.50 each, but now the price is $3.00 each. Write a sentence telling what you would expect buyers to do and explain why.

Activity 11.3 - (continued) **Assessment**

Read each of the problems below and answer the question. Show your work. You may draw a picture or diagram to show how you got the answer.

3. If your allowance is $1.75 a week, and the price of video games is $.25 per game, how many video games could you play in a week? Show your work.

____

____

____

____

4. If your allowance is $1.75 a week, and the price of video games increased to $.50 per game, how many video games could you play in a week? Show your work.

____

____

____

____

Activity 11.3 - (continued) **Assessment**

5. **When the price of video games increased in question #4, were you able to play more or fewer video games in a week? Why?**

____

____

____

____

Circle "more" or "less" to make the following statement true.

6. **The law of demand tells us that when the price of a good or service increases, consumers will buy (more/less) of the good or service, and when the price of a good or service decreases, consumers will buy (more/less) of the good or service.**

Lesson 12 - **Neighborhood Producers and Consumers**

LESSON DESCRIPTION

In this lesson, students examine the story of "The Little Red Hen" to determine the types of activities that make someone a producer or a consumer. Students extend their knowledge of producers and consumers by identifying occasions on which members of the community act in the roles of producers and consumers.

CONCEPTS

Consumers
Goods
Producers
Services

CONTENT STANDARD

Standard 1 – Scarcity

- **Benchmark 3 for 4th grade:** Goods are objects that can satisfy people's wants.
- **Benchmark 4 for 4th grade:** Services are actions that can satisfy people's wants.
- **Benchmark 8 for 4th grade:** People whose wants are satisfied by using goods and services are called consumers.
- **Benchmark 15 for 4th grade:** People who make goods and provide services are called producers.

OBJECTIVES

The students will:

1. Define consumer and producer.
2. Provide examples of consumers and producers.
3. Identify goods and services.

TIME REQUIRED

60-90 minutes

MATERIALS

- ✓ Visuals 12.1, 12.2, 12.3, 12.4 and 12.5
- ✓ Copies of Activities 12.1, 12.2, 12.3 and 12.4, cut apart to provide one producer card, one consumer card, one good card and one service card for each student
- ✓ One copy of Activity 12.5 for each student
- ✓ Two nametags for each student
- ✓ One sheet of construction paper for each pair of students
- ✓ Crayons
- ✓ Strip of crepe paper, adding machine tape, newsprint or other paper to represent a street on the bulletin board display of businesses

PROCEDURE

1. Ask the students if they recall the story of "The Little Red Hen." Allow them to tell the story in their own words. Display Visual 12.1 to help them remember the story.

2. Ask the students what they thought of the cat, the dog and the mouse in the story. ***They were lazy.***

3. Explain that **consumers** are people whose wants are satisfied by goods and services—in other words, a consumer is someone who uses a good or service. Some examples of consumers are people getting haircuts at a hair stylist's shop or people buying cars at an automobile dealership.

4. Explain that **producers** are people and firms that use resources to make goods and services—in other words, a producer is someone who makes a good or service. Some examples

of producers are people who cut hair at a hair stylist's shop or people working on an auto assembly line.

5. Remind the students that **goods** are things that people use and can touch. Ask the students for examples of goods. ***Examples might include anything that is tangible and is consumed, such as cars, apples and socks.***

6. Remind the students that **services** are activities that someone does for us. Ask the students for examples of services. ***Examples might include any type of activity that someone does for us, such as cutting hair, laundering clothes and repairing cars.***

7. Discuss the following:

   A. In the story, what was the good? ***The cake***

   B. Who was the consumer in the story? ***The little red hen***

   C. What did she consume? ***The cake***

   D. Who was the producer in the story? ***The little red hen***

   E. What did she produce? ***The cake***

8. Explain that the cat, the dog and the mouse were not interested in helping the little red hen in the story. Display Visual 12.2 and tell the students that this is a different version of the "The Little Red Hen."

9. After reading the revised version of the story, discuss the following:

   A. Whose work produced the tall, ripe wheat? ***The cat's***

   B. Whose work produced the cut wheat? ***The dog's***

   C. Whose work produced the flour? ***The mouse's***

   D. Whose work produced the cake? ***The little red hen's***

   E. Who were producers in the story? ***The cat, dog, mouse and little red hen***

   F. Who were consumers in the story? ***The cat, dog, mouse and little red hen***

10. Point out that the animals were both producers and consumers. Explain that there are many examples of producers and consumers in every neighborhood. Distribute one producer, consumer, good and service card to each student. Display Visual 12.3.

11. Read each of the statements from Visual 12.3, as listed below, to the students. After reading each statement, ask the question that follows. Tell the students to answer the questions by holding up the appropriate card. Practice by reading statement "A" and asking the students to answer the questions using their cards. Once the students understand how to follow the directions, proceed with the rest of the statements.

   A. Each Tuesday and Thursday, Ron's Trash Truck rolls through the neighborhood, stopping at every house to pick up the trash.

   Questions: Is Ron a producer or a consumer? ***Ron is a producer.*** Is trash pick-up a good or a service? ***It is a service.***

   B. One Thursday morning, Mrs. Able rushed out of her house and waved to Ron as he removed her trash.

   Questions: Is Mrs. Able a producer or a consumer? ***Mrs. Able is a consumer.*** Is she consuming a good or a service? ***She is consuming a service.***

   C. Mrs. Able hurried off to her job at the firehouse. Just as she arrived, she was called to save a cat that was stuck in a tree.

   Questions: Is Mrs. Able a producer or a consumer? ***Mrs. Able is a producer.*** Is she providing a good or a service? ***She is providing a service.***

   D. Mr. Baxter published a story about Mrs. Able in his newspaper, the ***Neighborhood Dispatch.***

   Questions: Is Mr. Baxter a producer or a

consumer? ***Mr. Baxter is a producer.*** Is the newspaper a good or a service? ***The newspaper is a good.***

E. William gathered the newspapers, put them in the basket on his handlebars, and rode around the neighborhood delivering papers to every home. He had just started working for Mr. Baxter.

Questions: Is William a producer or a consumer? ***William is a producer.*** Is newspaper delivery a good or a service? ***It is a service.***

F. William turned 10 years old on Thursday, and his mom surprised him with a new bike. William rode it around the block to try it out.

Questions: Is William a producer or a consumer? ***William is a consumer.*** Is the bike a good or a service? ***It is a good.***

G. The bike was specially built by Mike Cooper, who owns Mike's Custom Bike Shop.

Questions: Is Mike a producer or a consumer? ***Mike is a producer.*** Is a bike a good or a service? ***It is a good.***

H. William liked his new bike, but he received his best and most unexpected present early in the morning, when his cat was rescued from a tree.

Questions: When William's cat was rescued, was William a consumer or a producer? ***William was a consumer.*** Was the rescue a good or service? ***It was a service.***

12. Ask the students the following questions:
    A. Who saved William's cat? ***Mrs. Able***
    B. Mrs. Able was a producer and a consumer. When was Mrs. Able a producer in the story? ***Mrs. Able was a producer when she rescued the cat, when she was a firefighter.***
    C. When was Mrs. Able a consumer in the story? ***When Mrs. Able's trash was collected by Ron's Trash Truck***
    D. Who else was both a consumer and a producer in the story? ***William***
    E. In what ways was William a consumer? ***William received a bike. William's cat was rescued.***
    F. In what way was William a producer? ***William delivered newspapers.***

13. Remind the students that in the second version of the "Little Red Hen" story, the animals were both producers and consumers. Explain that most people are both consumers and producers. People produce a particular good or service to sell to consumers. They buy all of the other goods and services they want from other producers.

14. Ask the students to name 10 businesses on a main street in their community or to name 10 businesses in their community. Record the businesses on the board (For example, a bank, restaurant, dry cleaners, barber, hair salon, movie theater, car wash, dentist, doctor, grocery store or pharmacy).

15. Place the students in pairs. Give each pair of students a piece of construction paper. Instruct the students to fold the paper in half. In the top portion of the construction paper, tell each pair to draw a picture of one of the businesses listed on the board, making certain that each pair chooses a different business. Represent "Main Street" on the bulletin board by placing a strip of crepe paper, adding machine tape or newsprint on the bulletin board and placing the pictures of the businesses on both sides of the street in the order they occur on the street, if possible.

16. Give each student two nametags. On one of the tags, have the students write their own names. On the other, have the students write the name of an adult with whom they live.

17. Display Visual 12.4 and explain that the students will use it as a guide.

18. Have the students come to the board, one by one, and place their own nametags on the bottom portion of one of the pictures of a business they have visited. As the students place each nametag, have them state that they are consumers, the name of the product they consume, the name of the business from whom the product is purchased, and whether the product is a good or a service. Finally, the students should name the store as a producer.

19. When the students have finished placing their own names on the businesses, instruct them to repeat the process for the adult names they have written. Display Visual 12.5 and have the students refer to the visual as a guide.

20. After the students have placed all of the nametags on the bulletin board, ask the following questions of the class:

A. Who are some consumers in your neighborhood? ***The students should name people they know who use goods and services.***

B. Who are some producers in your neighborhood? ***The students should name people and businesses that make goods or perform services.***

C. Name a producer who is also a consumer. ***Most of the adults who consume goods and services also produce a good or service in their work. The students might also remember from the previous story that William and Mrs. Able were producers and consumers.***

D. Can you name a consumer who is also a producer? ***The adults who produce a good or service in their work also consume goods and services. The students might also remember from the previous story that William and Mrs. Able were producers and consumers.***

CLOSURE

21. Review the important points in the lesson by asking the following questions:

A. What is a producer? ***Someone who makes a good or a service***

B. Give an example of a producer. ***Students could state an occupation, such as a baker, a firefighter or a teacher. Students could state a business, such as a grocery store or hair salon.***

C. What is a consumer? ***Someone who uses a good or a service***

D. Give an example of a consumer. ***Students might name themselves or members of their families, or just state that everyone consumes.***

E. What is a good? ***Something tangible that you can use; something that you can touch and use***

F. Give an example of a good. ***A cake, a bike, and so on***

G. What is a service? ***An activity someone does for you***

H. Give an example of a service. ***Trash collecting, newspaper delivery, and so on***

I. How can an individual be both a consumer and a producer? ***Most people are both producers and consumers. People produce a good or service to sell, then they buy all of their other goods or services from other producers.***

ASSESSMENT

Distribute a copy of Activity 12.5 to each student. As homework, instruct the students to interview an adult in their household. When the interviews are complete, have each student present his or her interview to the class. After each question/answer, ask the students the following questions about the information they collected in the interview:

Interview Question	**Question for Student**
What is your name?	**When is** (name) **a producer?** *When (name) works at his or her job* **When is** (name) **a consumer?** *When he or she uses goods and services*
What grocery store do you like?	**Is** (grocery store) **a producer or consumer?** *Producer* **When the manager and workers work at the** (grocery store), **are they producers or consumers?** *Producers*
What vegetables do you buy at the grocery store?	**Are vegetables a good or a service?** *Good*
What do you buy at the hardware store?	**Is a** (hardware product) **a good or a service?** *Good*
Where do you get your hair cut?	**Is a haircut a good or a service?** *Service* **Is the hairdresser a consumer or producer?** *Producer*

Visual 12.1 - **The Story of the Little Red Hen**

Once upon a time, a cat, a dog, a mouse and a little red hen lived in the same neighborhood. The little red hen baked very good cakes, and she enjoyed producing them, but it was hard work producing them all by herself.

One day, she found some grains of wheat and asked her neighbors, "Who will help me plant this wheat?"

"Not I," said the cat. "Not I," said the dog. "Not I," said the mouse. So the little red hen planted the wheat all by herself.

When the wheat grew tall and ripe, the little red hen asked, "Who will help me cut the wheat?"

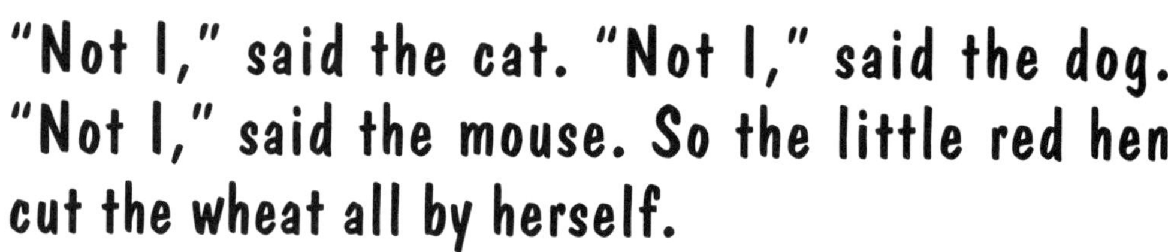

"Not I," said the cat. "Not I," said the dog. "Not I," said the mouse. So the little red hen cut the wheat all by herself.

The little red hen then asked, "Who will help me grind the wheat into flour?"

"Not I," said the cat. "Not I," said the dog. "Not I,"

Visual 12.1 - (continued)

The Story of the Little Red Hen

said the mouse. So the little red hen ground the wheat into flour all by herself.

Then, the little red hen mixed the flour with milk, sugar, eggs and butter. She poured the cake batter into a pan, and baked the cake until it was golden brown. The wonderful aroma filled the neighborhood.

The cat, the dog and the mouse noticed the wonderful smell and rushed out to visit the little red hen. The little red hen opened the door and greeted her three, hungry neighbors with a question, "Who will help me eat this cake?"

"I will," said the cat. "I will," said the dog. "I will," said the mouse.

But the little red hen shouted, "NO! You would not help me plant the wheat, you would not help me cut the wheat, and you would not help me grind the wheat into flour," she said.

So, the little red hen ate the cake all by herself. It was delicious!

Visual 12.2 - **A Nicer Story of the Little Red Hen**

Once upon a time, a cat, a dog, a mouse and a little red hen lived in the same neighborhood. The little red hen baked very good cakes, and she enjoyed producing them, but it was hard work producing them all by herself.

One day, she found some grains of wheat and asked her neighbors, "Who will help me plant this wheat?"

"I will," replied the cat. The cat planted the wheat.

When the wheat grew tall and ripe, the little red hen asked, "Who will help me cut the wheat?"

"I will," replied the dog. The dog cut the wheat.

The little red hen then asked, "Who will help me grind the wheat into flour?"

"I will," replied the mouse. The mouse ground the wheat into flour.

Visual 12.2 - (continued)
A Nicer Story of the Little Red Hen

When the wheat was delivered to the little red hen, she mixed it with milk, sugar, eggs and butter. She poured the cake batter into a pan and baked the cake until it was golden brown. The wonderful aroma filled the neighborhood.

The cat, the dog and the mouse noticed the wonderful smell and rushed out to visit the little red hen. The little red hen opened the door and greeted her three hungry neighbors with a question, "Who will help me eat this cake?"

"I will," said the cat. "I will," said the dog. "I will," said the mouse.

And they all ate the cake together. It was delicious!

Visual 12.3 - **A Day in the Neighborhood**

Each Tuesday and Thursday, Ron's Trash Truck rolls through the neighborhood, stopping at every house to pick up the trash.

One Thursday morning, Mrs. Able rushed out of her house and waved to Ron as he removed her trash.

Mrs. Able hurried off to her job at the firehouse. Just as she arrived, she was called to save a cat that was stuck in a tree.

Mr. Baxter published a story about Mrs. Able in his newspaper, the *Neighborhood Dispatch*.

William gathered the newspapers, put them

Visual 12.3 - (continued)

A Day in the Neighborhood

in the basket on his handlebars, and rode around the neighborhood, delivering papers to every home. He had just started working for Mr. Baxter.

William turned 10 years old on Thursday, and his mom surprised him with a new bike. William rode it around the block to try it out.

The bike was specially built by Mike Cooper, who owns Mike's Custom Bike Shop.

William liked his new bike, but he received his best and most unexpected present early in the morning when his cat was rescued from a tree.

Visual 12.4 - **Student Consumers**

I am a consumer.

I buy ______________________ at
(Name of product)

______________________ .
(Name of business)

____
(Name of product)
is/are a (good or service).

____
(Name of business)
is a producer.

Visual 12.5 - **Adult Consumers**

____
(Name of adult) is a consumer.

He or she buys ____________________ at
(Name of product)

____________________ .
(Name of business)

____
(Name of product)

is/are a (good or service).

____
(Name of business)

is a producer.

Activity 12.1 - **Producer Cards**

Producer	**Producer**
Producer	**Producer**

Activity 12.2 - **Consumer Cards**

Consumer	Consumer
Consumer	Consumer

Activity 12.3 - **Good Cards**

Good	Good
Good	Good

Activity 12.4 - **Service Cards**

Service	Service
Service	Service

Activity 12.5 - **Assessment**

Interview an adult in your home. Ask the adult each of the questions and write the answers in the space provided.

What is your name?

____

What grocery store do you like?

____

What vegetables do you buy at the grocery store?

____

What do you buy at the hardware store?

____

Where do you get your hair cut?

____

Lesson 13 - **Moving in Economic Circles**

LESSON DESCRIPTION

In this lesson, the students experience the circular flow of economic activity by assuming the roles of households and businesses and seeking to make exchanges in both the market for resources and the market for goods and services. This lesson assumes prior knowledge of goods, services and resources.

CONCEPTS

Circular flow
Consumers
Producers

CONTENT STANDARDS

Standard 7 – Markets – Price and Quantity Determination

- **Benchmark 2 for 4th grade:** A market exists whenever buyers and sellers exchange goods and services.
- **Benchmark 3 for 4th grade:** Most people both produce and consume. As producers they make goods and services; as consumers they use goods and services.

Standard 11 – Role of Money

- **Benchmark 3 for 4th grade:** People consume goods and services, not money; money is useful primarily because it can be used to buy goods and services.
- **Benchmark 4 for 4th grade:** Producers use natural resources, human resources and capital goods (not money) to make goods and services.

Standard 13 – Role of Resources in Determining Income

- **Benchmark 1 for 4th grade:** Labor is a human resource used to produce goods and services.
- **Benchmark 2 for 4th grade:** People can earn income by exchanging their human resources (Physical or mental work) for wages or salaries.
- **Benchmark 1 for 8th grade:** Employers are willing to pay wages and salaries to workers because they expect to sell the goods and services those workers produce at prices high enough to cover the wages and salaries and all other costs of production.
- **Benchmark 2 for 8th grade:** To earn income, people sell productive resources. These include their labor, capital, natural resources, and entrepreneurial talents.

OBJECTIVES

The students will:

1. Explain that businesses are consumers of resources and producers of goods and services.
2. Explain that households and individuals are consumers of goods and services and producers of resources.
3. Identify revenue as the return businesses receive for selling goods and services.
4. Identify wages as the return households and individuals receive for selling their human resources.
5. Give examples of markets in which buyers and sellers meet face-to-face and other markets in which buyers and sellers never meet.

TIME REQUIRED

60-90 minutes

MATERIALS

✓ Construction-paper signs, as follows: "Households and Individuals," "Businesses," "Market

for Goods and Services," "Market for Resources," "Resource Owners," "Consumers of Goods and Services," "Consumers of Resources," "Producers of Goods and Services"
- ✓ Construction-paper sign: "Production," tied with yarn to hang around the teacher's neck
- ✓ Activity 13.1, cut apart to provide one card per student
- ✓ Activity 13.2, cut apart to provide one card per student
- ✓ Copies of Activity 13.3, cut apart to provide:
  - Money Cards (for one-half of the students)
  - Resource Cards (for one-half of the students)
  - Good or Service Cards (for one-half of the students)
- ✓ One copy of Activity 13.4 for each student
- ✓ Visual 13.1
- ✓ Masking tape
- ✓ Picture of a car, either drawn and cut out or cut from a photograph

PROCEDURE

Day 1

1. Before beginning the lesson, place four of the signs on the walls of the room, as follows:
   - Market for Goods and Services (on north wall)
   - Businesses (east wall)
   - Market for Resources (south wall)
   - Households and Individuals (west wall)

2. Begin the lesson by explaining that there are many people who participate in the economy. In fact, even the students participate. Ask the students if they can state ways they participate in the economy. ***Students should state that they have purchased goods and services.***

3. Explain that they participate in the economy as individuals. They and everyone in their homes participate in the economy by buying goods and services.

4. Explain that households and individuals are one very large group in our society that participates in the economy. Imagine a circle on the board and draw a box on the left side of the circle (at the "nine o'clock" position). Write "Households and Individuals" in the box (see example).

Households and Individuals

5. Ask the students for examples of the goods and services they buy. As they name products, record the list on the board, well away from the imagined circular area.

6. After listing approximately 10 products, explain that these products are produced by businesses. Explain that businesses are another large group that operates in our economy. Draw a box on the right side of the imagined circle (at the "three o'clock" position) and label it "Businesses." The diagram on the board will then look like the example below:

Households and Individuals	Businesses

7. Move one-by-one down the list of goods and services the students have named and ask the students where they bought these goods and services. Record their answers on the board – again, well away from the imagined circle. ***Answers will vary. Students will have purchased most of their goods and services at a store; however, some may say they purchased an item online or that they bought it from a catalog or a newspaper ad.***

8. Explain that goods and services move from

businesses to households and individuals easily in our economy. Goods and services follow an imaginary path to a market. Draw a box at the top of the circle and label it as "Market for Goods and Services." The diagram should now look like the example below:

	Market for Goods and Services	
Households and Individuals		Businesses

9. Ask the students for examples of markets. The students should state all of those places listed on the board. Explain that markets do not have to be a place. Ask the following questions.

   A. What goods have you purchased from a grocery store? ***Answers will vary.***

   B. Is a grocery store a market? ***Yes***

   C. Name someone you know who has purchased a good online. (If the students do not know anyone who has made a purchase, describe a purchase you have made from an online catalog or store.)

   D. Can you name some online stores? ***Amazon, Barnes and Noble, eBay, Overstock, Target, others***

   E. Where is your grocery store? Describe what it looks like. ***Answers will vary.***

   F. Have you purchased goods at a mall? Where is the mall? Describe what it looks like. ***Answers will vary.***

   G. Where is Amazon? Describe what it looks like. ***The students will be unable to describe an Amazon location.***

   H. Where is eBay? Describe what it looks like. ***The students will be unable to describe an eBay location.***

10. Explain that the students have just discussed many types of markets for goods and services. Some are places where a buyer sees the seller face-to-face. In some markets, buyers do not see sellers.

11. Explain that consumers buy and use goods and services. This means that all of the students and all of the others in their households are consumers. Ask the students if the adults in their households or in their neighborhoods participate in the economy in any ways other than as consumers. ***The students should recognize that the adults in their households or neighborhoods work in the economy.***

12. Discuss the following:

    A. Name some of the places where adults you know work. ***The students should name local businesses.*** List the students' answers on the board.(**NOTE:** Some students will name government offices and schools. For purposes of this activity we will categorize these as businesses.)

    B. At what stores have you noticed adults working? ***Answers will vary.*** Add these answers to the list on the board.

13. Point out that the list includes many businesses where adults work. Remind the students that businesses make and sell goods and services. Explain that businesses get people to make and sell the goods and services from households. Discuss the following:

    A. What is the economic term to describe people working? ***Human resources***

    B. Can you think of ways that businesses find human resources and human resources find businesses? ***Answers will vary.***

14. Point out that people answer employment ads in newspapers or online. Sometimes a friend tells someone that a business is looking for workers. Many businesses list the jobs they have available on their Web site.

15. Explain that these are all paths for workers to

get to businesses. All of these paths go through the Market for Resources. Draw a box at the bottom of the imagined circle and label it "Market for Resources."

Market for Goods and Services

Households and Individuals

Businesses

Market for Resources

16. Using the cut-out picture of a car, begin at the "Businesses" box and illustrate the flow of goods, services and resources through the economy as follows:

A. The car factory is a business that produces cars. Is a car a good or a service? ***Good***

B. Where are the cars going? ***To households and individuals***

C. How do the cars get from the businesses to households and individuals? ***Through the market for goods and services***

17. Draw an arrow from "Businesses" to "Households and Individuals." Make sure that the arrow goes through the "Market for Goods and Services." Continue the discussion as follows:

A. Households and individuals buy goods and services.

B. What do households and individuals sell? ***If students answer "workers," restate it as "human resources."***

18. Beginning at "Households and Individuals," draw an arrow that goes through the "Market for Resources" to "Businesses." Ask the students why the path to "Businesses" is through the "Market for Resources." ***Students should state that this market is where human resources find businesses and businesses find human resources.***

19. Explain that all of the things that follow the paths of the arrows are real things – that is, things we can physically touch or physical actions we can observe. Discuss the following:

- The arrow from "Businesses" to "Households and Individuals" shows the path that cars, cereal, video games, haircuts, automobiles and taxi rides take to get from businesses to households and individuals.
- The arrow from "Households and Individuals" to "Businesses" shows the path the human resources take. Goods and services, such as cars and haircuts, are real. Human resources are real. So, this circular path is called the "real flow." See diagram below.

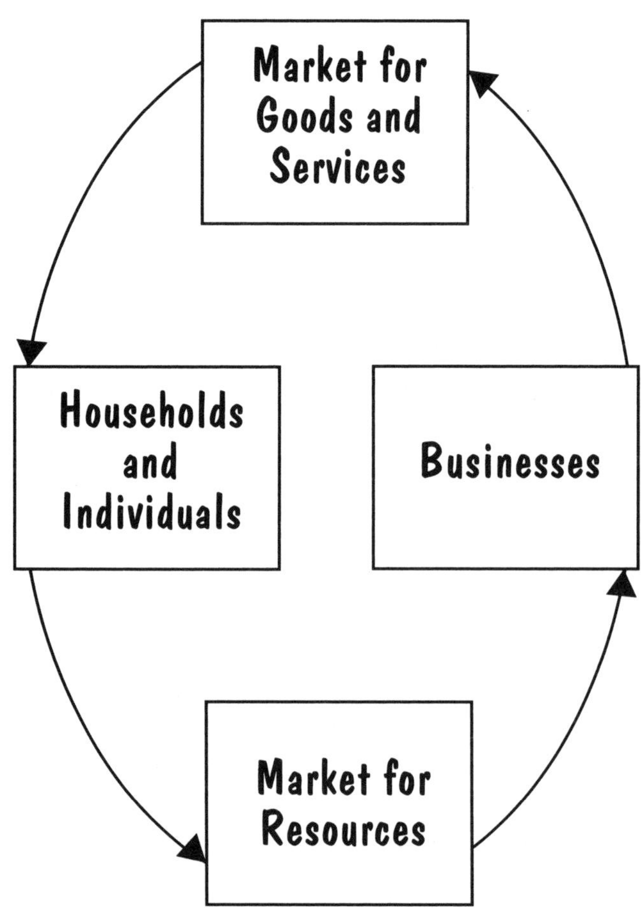

Day 2

20. Ask the students to name some goods they buy in the market for goods and services. ***Answers will vary.*** Choose one of the students who recently purchased a small good, and ask the following questions:

A. Where did you buy the item? ***Answers will vary.***

B. What did the clerk say to you when you took the (name the good) to the counter? ***Answers will vary, but might include, "Did you find everything you were looking for?" "Is there anything else we can help you find?" "Will this be all?"*** If the student responds by saying that the clerk stated the price, skip to step 22. If the student does not mention the price, continue with the next question.

C. Did the clerk put your purchase in a bag? ***Answers will vary.***

21. Make the following statement: So, you took the (name of good) to the counter, the clerk said (repeat student's statement), the clerk placed your item in a bag, and then you left the store. Ask if anything else happened. ***The student should mention that he or she paid for the item.*** If the student has not mentioned payment, ask the other students if they think something else might have happened that (student's name) has forgotten. ***Payment***

22. Explain that two things happen in the Market for Goods and Services: Households and Individuals get goods and services such as cars, cereal and haircuts, and Businesses get revenue. Revenue is the money payment for goods and services. The money moves from Households and Individuals to Businesses through the Market for Goods and Services. Draw an arrow going from "Households and Individuals" to "Businesses," through the "Market for Goods and Services" (clockwise). Place dollar signs along the arrow. Discuss the following:

A. Name some people who work for businesses. ***Answers will vary.***

B. What do people who work for businesses receive for their work? ***Money***

23. Explain that the money that people get in exchange for work is called wages or salaries. This money is their income. The money goes from the Businesses to the Households and Individuals through the Market for Resources. Draw an arrow going from "Businesses" to "Households and Individuals," through the "Market for Resources" (clockwise). Place dollar signs along the arrow. See diagram below.

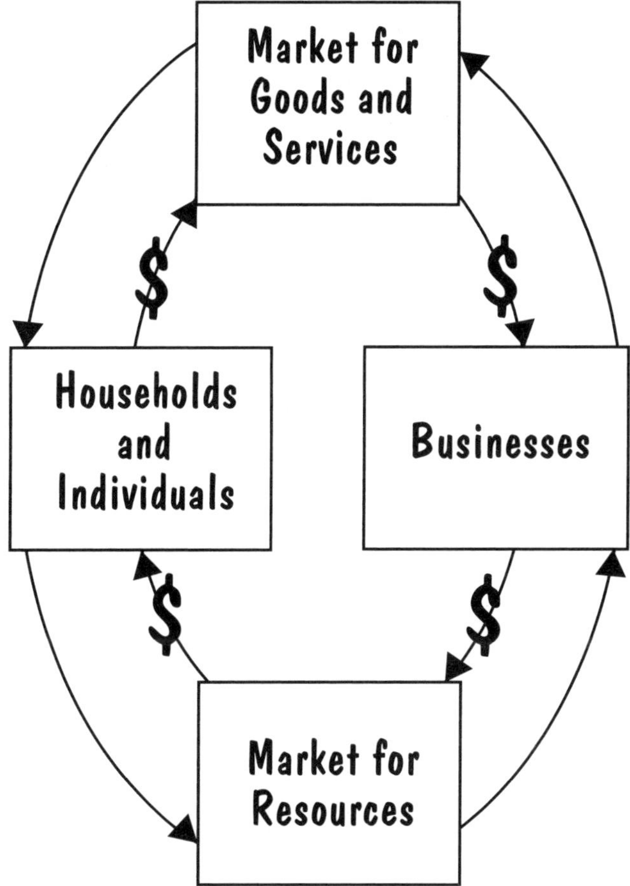

24. Explain that the circle with the dollar signs is called the money flow. Remind the students that the circle with the goods, services and resources (counter-clockwise) is referred to as the real flow. Ask the students why this is called the real flow. ***Real things move from Households and Individuals to Businesses—resources. And, real things move from Businesses to Households and Individuals—goods and services.*** The other circle shows the direction of the money as Households and Individuals and Businesses pay for the goods, services and resources.

25. Explain that the students are going to participate in a role play. They will act as Household and Individuals and as Businesses and find others with whom to exchange goods, services and resources. Tell the students that they will receive cards that tell them what roles they will take.

26. Place students in two groups of equal size. Distribute a card from Activity 13.1 to each student. The cards are matched as buyer and seller, side-by-side on the activity sheets. Give those students acting as Businesses the "A" cards, and those acting as Household and Individuals the "B" cards. Do not mention the purpose of the A-B coding to the students. Place the "Good or Service" cards, the "Resource" cards and the "Money" cards from Activity 13.2 in stacks on a desk or table. Place some of the "Instruction Cards for Market for Goods and Services" from Activity 13.3 on a desk or table. Explain the following:

- Each student is in one of two groups in the economy—either the "Households and Individuals" group or the "Businesses" group.
- If the student's role is that he or she is looking for a job, the student should pick a "Resource" card from the table.
- If the student's role is that he or she is a business that wants to hire a human resource, the student should pick up a "Money" card from the table in order to pay the human resources.
- After choosing a card, each student should go to the group (the sign on the wall) where he or she belongs.

27. Go to the Households and Individuals group and discuss the following:

- Are any of you looking for a human resource to work for your business? ***The answer should be "no."***
- Businesses are the group that hires human resources. Human resources are in the Households and Individuals group.
- If students are looking for a human resource, they should go to the Businesses group.

28. Go to the Businesses group and discuss the following:

- Are any of you trying to find a job? ***The answer should be "no."***
- The students looking for a job are human resources.
- Businesses buy the work of human resources from Households and Individuals.
- If students are trying to find a job, they should go to the Households and Individuals group.

29. Point to the two "Market" signs on the wall.

- If a student is trying to find a job, he or she should go to the appropriate market to find someone who is offering the job that the student wants, and give someone in that market group his or her resource card in exchange for a money card as payment.
- If a student is trying to hire a human resource, he or she should go to the appropriate market to find someone who wants to do the kind of work the student is offering. The student should collect a resource card in exchange for payment—the money card.

30. Put the "Production" sign on. Explain that production takes place when businesses use resources to make goods and services. Stand under the "Businesses" sign.

- Instruct the students that if they represent a business and have purchased a human resource in the resource market, they should return to the business group and give the teacher the "Resource" card.
- Explain to the students that the "Resource" cards will be used to produce goods and services. Explain that the teacher will take the resource card and give the students a "Goods and Services" card and an "Instruction" card for the Market for Goods and Services.

(**NOTE:** Use only the "A" cards from Activity 13.3. Be sure that each student receives a good or service that is consistent with the business he or she represents by matching the symbols in the upper left corner of the cards.)

- Explain that once the students have

their cards, they will sell their good or service by finding someone who wants to buy it in the Market for Goods and Services.

- Instruct the students representing Households and Individuals to pick up an "Instruction" card for the Market for Goods and Services and go to the Market for Goods and Services to purchase the item on the card. Provide each of these students with a "B" card from Activity 13.3.
- When the students find a business that is selling what they want to buy, they should take the "Good or Service" card from the business and give the business a "Money" card.
- When the students have traded cards, they should return to their group.

31. When the students have returned to their groups, ask the following questions:

A. Besides the instruction card, what card do Households and Individuals have? "***Goods and Services" card***

B. How did the Households and Individuals get the Goods and Services? ***They went to the Market for Goods and Services and purchased their good or service from a business.***

C. Where did the businesses get the goods and services they sold? ***They produced them.***

D. Where did the businesses get the resources they used to produce the goods and services? ***They purchased the resources in the Market for Resources.***

E. Who sold the resources to the businesses? ***Households and Individuals***

F. Are resources real things? ***Yes***

G. Are goods and services real things? ***Yes***

H. Which way were the real things flowing in the exercise? ***Counter-clockwise***

CLOSURE

32. Instruct a student to "walk" the flow of real things. Prompt the student's movement by asking him or her the following questions:

A. Where did resources start? ***The student should stand at the "Households and Individuals" area.***

B. Where did the resources go after leaving the Households and Individuals? ***The student should move to the "Market for Resources."***

C. (To the class) What happened in the Market for Resources? ***Businesses purchased the resources.***

D. Where did the resources go when businesses purchased them? ***The student should move to the "Businesses" sign.***

E. (To the class) What happened to the resources when they went to the businesses? ***The resources were used to produce goods and services.***

F. Where did the goods and services go after the businesses produced them? ***The student should move to the "Market for Goods and Services."***

G. (To the class) What happened in the Market for Goods and Services? ***Households and Individuals purchased the goods and services.***

H. Where did the goods and services go after they were purchased? ***The student should move to the "Households and Individuals" sign.***

33. Point out that the student is back where he or she started. The flow of real things goes in a circle, just as the student did.

34. Explain that you have four signs left over. Show the students the "Resource Owners," "Consumers of Goods and Services," "Consumers of Resources" and "Producers of Goods and Services" signs. Explain that two of these signs describe Businesses and two of them describe Households and Individuals. Distribute the signs to four students. Have the four students come forward and tape their signs near the "Businesses" sign or the "Households and Individuals" sign, whichever is appropriate. ***The students should tape the "Resource Owners" and "Consumers of Goods and Services" signs near the "Households and Individuals" sign. The students should tape the "Consumers of Resources" and***

"Producers of Goods and Services" signs near the "Businesses" sign.

35. Explain that businesses are consumers when they purchase and use human resources and other resources. Discuss the following:

A. What do businesses do with the human resources they hire? ***The human resources are used to produce goods and services.***

B. What card are businesses holding? ***Money***

36. Instruct a student to "walk" the flow of money. Prompt the student's movement by asking the following questions of the student or the class:

A. In our activity, where did the money start? ***The student should stand at the "Businesses" sign.***

B. Where did the money go after leaving the business? ***The student should move to the "Market for Resources."***

C. (To the class) What happened in the Market for Resources? ***Households and Individuals sold their resources to Businesses.***

D. Where did the money go when Households and Individuals sold their resources? ***The student should move to the "Households and Individuals" sign.***

E. (To the class) What happened to the money when it went to the Households and Individuals? ***The Households and Individuals used it to buy goods and services.***

F. Where did Households and Individuals buy the goods and services? ***The student should move to the "Market for Goods and Services."***

G. (To the class) What happened in the Market for Goods and Services? ***Households and Individuals spent the money on goods and services.***

H. Where did the money go after the Households and Individuals spent it? ***The student should move to the "Businesses" sign.***

37. Point out that the student is back where he or she started. The flow of money goes in a circle, just as the student did.

(**NOTE:** Households and individuals provide other resources in the market for resources. These include natural resources, capital resources and entrepreneurial ability. Businesses consume these resources through the market for resources. Businesses pay costs of production for these resources, which become income in the form of rent [natural resources], interest [capital resources] and profit [entrepreneurial ability].

The means of transferring capital, natural, and entrepreneurial resources is complex, and the explanation is too complicated to present to students in third through fifth grade. For simplicity, this lesson refers to human resources only.")

ASSESSMENT

Place the students in pairs. Display Visual 13.1 and give each pair of students a copy of Activity 13.4. Tell the students to use the picture of the circular flow on the transparency to help them answer the questions on the handout.

Answers:

A. Who are the producers of goods and services? ***Businesses***

B. Who are the consumers of goods and services? ***Households and individuals***

C. Are goods and services real things, or are they money? ***Real things***

D. Do goods and services flow from the businesses to the households and individuals, or do goods and services flow from households and individuals to businesses? ***Goods and services flow from businesses to households and individuals.***

E. Who are the consumers of (human) resources? ***Businesses***

F. Who are the producers of (human) resources? ***Households and individuals***

G. Are resources real things or are they money? ***Real things***

H. Do resources flow from the businesses

to the households and individuals, or do resources flow from households and individuals to businesses? ***Resources flow from households and individuals to businesses.***

I. Where do businesses find human resources to produce goods and services? ***In the market for resources***

J. Where do human resources find jobs with businesses? ***In the market for resources***

K. What are some ways that businesses find human resources and human resources find businesses in the market for resources? ***On the company's Web site, in the newspaper, from a friend***

L. Where do households and individuals get goods and services? ***In the market for goods and services***

M. Where do businesses sell goods and services? ***In the market for goods and services***

N. What are some ways that households and individuals buy, and businesses sell, goods and services? ***Business Web sites, eBay, stores, catalogs***

O. How do households and individuals pay for goods and services? ***They pay money to businesses.***

P. How do businesses pay for human resources? ***They pay wages to human resources.***

Visual 13.1 - **Circular Flow**

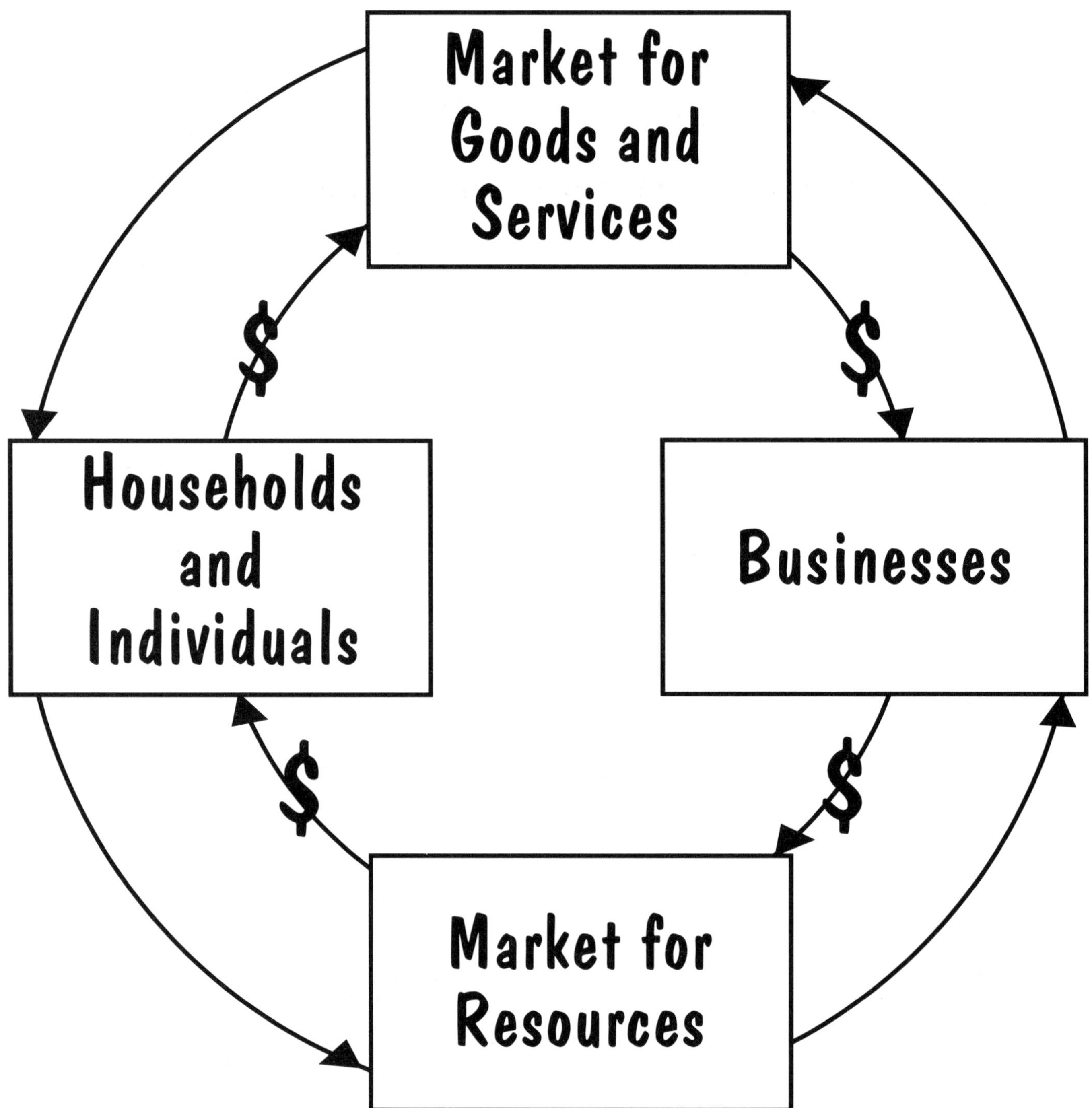

Activity 13.1 - **Instruction Cards for Market for Resources**

A	B
 Flameglow Candles wants to hire someone to answer the phones and take orders for candles.	Ronald just got out of high school and wants an office job helping customers by phone. He does not want to work on Saturdays.

A	B
 Flameglow Candles wants to hire someone to design scented candles.	Susie's hobby has been designing candles. She wants to find a job designing candles.

Activity 13.1 - **Instruction Cards for Market for Resources**

A  **The Big Ball Business is looking for a human resource with graphic art experience to design happy faces on balls.**	**B** **Joe has graphic art experience and is looking for a job.**
A  **Big Ball Business is looking for a human resource who knows how to organize an office.**	**B** **James just completed school, where he learned how to file things and how to keep an office organized by using a computer. He is looking for a job in an office.**

Activity 13.1 - (continued) **Instruction Cards for Market for Resources**

A	B
 Cakery Bakery is looking for a human resource that knows all about keeping a workspace clean and germ-free. The job is posted on the Cakery Bakery Web site.	Marla has never worked before, but she has lots of experience cleaning her own spotless home. She is looking for a job.
A  Cakery Bakery would like to hire a human resource who knows how to bake cakes. The job is posted on the Cakery Bakery Web site.	**B** Robert just graduated from a school where he learned how to bake cakes and pastries. He is looking for a job.

Activity 13.1 - (continued) **Instruction Cards for Market for Resources**

A

Fly Ball, Inc. is a batting cage company that is looking for a human resource who knows how to repair pitching machines. Fly Ball, Inc. placed a "Help Wanted" ad in the newspaper.

B

Randy went to school to learn about machine repair and maintenance. He likes sports and is looking for a job at a sports company.

A

Fly Ball, Inc. is looking for a human resource who can answer the phones on Saturdays and help people make appointments for the batting cages. Fly Ball, Inc. placed a "Help Wanted" ad in the newspaper.

B

John is a student who would like to work on Saturdays.

Activity 13.1 - (continued) **Instruction Cards for Market for Resources**

A  Dr. Coats is looking for an assistant who can take his patients' temperatures and look in their ears and throats. She called a training school to get names of recent graduates.	**B** Keesha just completed school as a physician's assistant and wants to work in a doctor's office taking patients' temperatures and looking in their ears and throats.
A 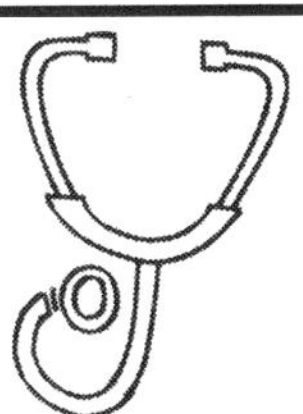 Dr. Coats is looking for a human resource who can answer the phone and make appointments. She placed an ad in the newspaper.	**B** The doctor that Marlyce worked for just retired. Marlyce wants to work for another doctor. She has experience answering the phones and making appointments.

Activity 13.1 - (continued) **Instruction Cards for Market for Resources**

A	B
 Shiney Pipe Company would like to hire a plumber to do home plumbing repair. They placed an ad in the newspaper.	Terrence just completed training as a plumber and is looking for his first job.
A	**B**
 Model Home, Inc. is looking for a carpenter to join its home remodeling staff. They placed an ad online.	Jana is a carpenter who is looking for a job in remodeling work.

Activity 13.2 - **Market Cards**

Good or Service	Good or Service
Good or Service	Good or Service
Good or Service	Good or Service
Good or Service	Good or Service

Activity 13.2 - (continued) **Market Cards**

Resource	Resource
Resource	Resource
Resource	Resource
Resource	Resource

Activity 13.2 - (continued) **Market Cards**

Money	Money
Money	Money
Money	Money
Money	Money

Activity 13.3 - **Instruction Cards for Market for Goods and Services**

A Flameglow Candles sells rose-scented candles.	**B** You would like to buy a candle that smells like vanilla or flowers.
A  Flameglow Candles sells candles in five different shades of pink.	**B** You would like to buy a pink candle.

Activity 13.3 - (continued) **Instruction Cards for Market for Goods and Services**

<table>
<tr>
<td>

A

The Big Ball Business is selling a happy-face ball.

</td>
<td>

B

You would like to buy a happy-face ball for your brother.

</td>
</tr>
<tr>
<td>

A

The Big Ball Business is selling a happy-face ball.

</td>
<td>

B

Your friend wants a happy-face ball for her birthday.

</td>
</tr>
</table>

Activity 13.3 - (continued) **Instruction Cards for Market for Goods and Services**

A	B
A  Cakery Bakery is selling a birthday cake.	B You want to buy a birthday cake for your mom.
A  Cakery Bakery is selling cakes decorated for graduation.	B You want to buy a cake for your brother's graduation.

Activity 13.3 - (continued) **Instruction Cards for Market for Goods and Services**

A Fly Ball, Inc. is selling 30-minute batting cage specials for $3.00.	**B** You want to buy some time in the batting cages.
A  Fly Ball, Inc. is selling 60-minute batting cage specials for $5.00.	**B** You want to buy some time in the batting cages.

Activity 13.3 - (continued) **Instruction Cards for Market for Goods and Services**

A	B
 Dr. Coats takes care of people who have the flu.	You don't feel well. You need to see the doctor.
A	B
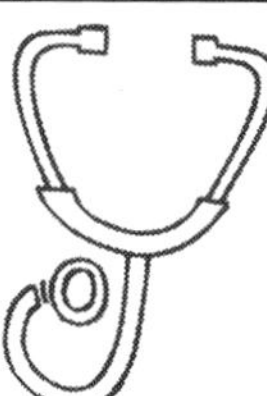 Dr. Coats gives measles shots.	You need to get a measles booster shot.

Activity 13.3 - (continued) **Instruction Cards for Market for Goods and Services**

A Model Home, Inc. sells kitchen remodeling.	**B** You want your kitchen remodeled.
A Shiney Pipe Company repairs sink faucets.	**B** The faucet in your bathroom is leaking, and you want to find someone to fix it.

Activity 13.4 - **Assessment**

Use the circular flow drawing on the Visual to help you answer the following questions.

A. Who are the producers of goods and services?

____

B. Who are the consumers of goods and services?

____

C. Are goods and services real things, or are they money?

____

D. Do goods and services flow from the businesses to the households and individuals, or do goods and services flow from households and individuals to businesses?

____

E. Who are the consumers of (human) resources?

____

F. Who are the producers of (human) resources?

____

Activity 13.4 - (continued) **Assessment**

G. Are resources real things, or are they money?

____

H. Do resources flow from the businesses to the households and individuals, or do resources flow from households and individuals to businesses?

____

I. Where do businesses find human resources to produce goods and services?

____

J. Where do human resources find jobs with businesses?

____

K. What are some ways that businesses find human resources and human resources find businesses in the market for resources?

____

L. Where do households and individuals get goods and services?

____

Activity 13.4 - (continued) **Assessment**

M. Where do businesses sell goods and services?

____

N. What are some ways that households and individuals buy, and businesses sell, goods and services?

____

O. How do households and individuals pay for goods and services?

____

P. How do businesses pay for human resources?

____

Lesson 14 - **Tic-Tac-Toe Trade**

LESSON DESCRIPTION

In this lesson, the students participate in an activity that demonstrates the benefits of specialization and voluntary exchange. The students are divided into two groups, representing two countries, and the students in each country produce "X's" and "O's" for their country's national sport, Tic-Tac-Toe. Then, the students are asked to specialize by producing only X's or O's. Finally, they are asked to trade.

CONCEPTS

Interdependence
Specialization
Trade

CONTENT STANDARDS

Content Standard 5 – Trade

- **Benchmark 6 for 8th Grade:** Voluntary exchange among people or organizations in different countries gives people a broader range of choices in buying goods and services.

Content Standard 6 – Specialization

- **Benchmark 1 for 4th Grade:** Economic specialization occurs when people concentrate their production on fewer kinds of goods and services than they consume.
- **Benchmark 4 for 4th Grade:** Greater specialization leads to increased interdependence among producers and consumers.

OBJECTIVES

The students will:

1. Define economic specialization.

2. Explain that specialization increases interdependence.

3. Recognize that trade allows countries to consume more than they can produce.

TIME REQUIRED

45-60 minutes

MATERIALS

✓ Two pipe cleaners per student, to be twisted into the shape of "O's" and "X's" for the game – one whole pipe cleaner for each "O" and one pipe cleaner cut in half for each "X."
 ✦ Give each student in Gameland two whole pipe cleaners.
 ✦ Give each student in Playland four half pipe cleaners.
✂ Scissors
✓ Visuals 14.1, 14.2, 14.3 and 14.4
✓ One copy of Activity 14.1 for each student
✓ (Optional) Pieces of cardboard, with Tic-Tac-Toe grids drawn on each
✓ (Optional) Prizes for winners of Tic-Tac-Toe

PROCEDURE

1. Ask the students if they have ever traded something (like a toy) with a friend. ***Most will answer "yes."*** Ask them what they traded and what they received in return. ***Sandwiches at lunch, baseball cards, toys*** Ask them why they traded. ***To get something they didn't have but that they wanted*** Define **trade** as exchanging goods, services and resources for other goods, services and resources, or for money.

2. Explain that if people in the United States weren't able to trade with people in other countries, they wouldn't have products such as chocolate, diamonds, bananas and even aluminum soda cans.

3. Explain that in this lesson they will learn that trade allows people to have more products than they are able to make on their own.

4. Tell the students that when people in one country specialize, it means that people in that country produce the things that they can make well. **Specialization** occurs when people make only a few of the goods and services that they consume.

5. Tell the students that when a country specializes and trades with other countries, more can be produced, and each country can have more goods and services to consume. However, greater specialization leads to increased interdependence. **Interdependence** means that people must depend on other people to get what they want.

6. Explain that this lesson will help the students understand how countries that specialize and trade can have more goods and services than if they tried to make everything on their own.

7. Divide the students into two groups of equal size. Explain that the students in the first group are citizens in the country "Gameland," and the students in the second group are citizens in the country "Playland."

8. Tell the students that they are going to be workers in their countries. The students in both countries will produce "X's" and "O's" for their country's favorite sport, Tic-Tac-Toe. Because roughly an equal number of X's and O's are needed to play Tic-Tac-Toe, the more sets of X's and O's a country has, the more of its people can play the game. Each set consists of one X and one O.

9. Distribute only whole pipe cleaners to the students in Gameland. Give each student two pipe cleaners. Tell the Gameland students that each worker can make either two O's or one X. Demonstrate how to produce X's and O's.
   - To form each "O," shape one whole pipe cleaner into a circle, twisting the ends together to hold the shape.
   - To form each "X," fold the two pipe cleaners together in the middle and bend to form and hold the "X" shape.

   Tell the students that each of them must decide whether to produce two O's or one X, keeping in mind that people in their country need sets of O's and X's to play. Help the students notice that it is easier for them to make O's than X's with their resources.

10. Distribute four half pipe cleaners to each student in Playland. Tell the students that each worker can make either two X's or one O. Demonstrate as follows:
    - To form each "O," twist the four pieces together, then twist the ends together to hold the shape.
    - To form each "X," fold each half of the pipe cleaners in half and hook the two pieces together at the folds. Twist to hold the two pieces together.

    Tell the students that each of them must decide whether to produce one O or two X's, keeping in mind that people in their country need sets of O's and X's to play. Help the students notice that it is easier for them to make X's than O's with their resources.

11. Display Visual 14.1, showing the following information:

    Each worker in Gameland can produce either
    2 O's or 1 X

    Each worker in Playland can produce either
    1 O or 2 X's

12. When the students have completed making X's and O's, have them count the total number of X's and O's produced in each country. Record the following information on Visual 14.2.
    - The number of X's and O's produced by each country
    - The number of sets produced by each country. A set is a pair consisting of one X and one O. The number of X's produced or the number of O's produced–whichever is low-

er–will equal the number of sets, and there may be either some X's or some O's that are not part of a set.

• The total number of sets. This is the sum of each country's number of sets, assuming no trade–i.e., extra X's from one country cannot be matched with extra O's from the other country.

13. Collect all the produced X's and O's.

14. Ask the students how they might increase the number of sets produced within their country. ***By making different production decisions if there are "extra" X's or O's***

15. Explain that workers in Gameland and Playland will now specialize. Ask the students what specialization means. ***People making only a few of the goods and services they consume*** Explain that the workers in Gameland will produce only O's and the workers in Playland will produce only X's. Each worker in Gameland will produce two O's, and each worker in Playland will produce two X's.

16. Distribute half pipe cleaners to the students in Playland (four half pipe cleaners to each student) and whole pipe cleaners to the students in Gameland (two pipe cleaners to each student).

17. Allow five minutes for the students to work. Have the students count the total number of X's or O's produced in each country. Record the following on Visual 14.3.

• The number of X's and O's produced by each country

• The number of sets produced by each country ***This will be zero, although the total number of X's and O's produced will be greater than in round one.***

18. Discuss the following questions:

A. When the workers in each country produced both X's and O's, how many of each were produced? ***The total number of each produced by both countries***

B. How many X's and how many O's were produced when the workers in each country specialized? ***The total number of O's produced by workers in Gameland; The total number of X's produced by workers in Playland***

C. Why could people in Gameland and Playland have more of both the second time they produced? ***Because workers in each country specialized and produced only one item, either X's or O's, that they were relatively better at producing***

D. Note that more were produced not just because workers specialized, but also because they specialized in doing the things they can do well and that entail the least sacrifice in forgone opportunities. Had they specialized the other way around — that is, Gameland producing X's and Playland producing O's — less would have been produced.

19. (Optional) Tell the students in each country that there are boards so that they can play Tic-Tac-Toe, and that they will have time to play with the pieces they just produced.

20. Ask the students if there is a problem with playing the game in their country. ***Of course there will be a problem, because Gameland only has O's and Playland only has X's—they do not have sets.*** Discuss the following questions:

A. People in Gameland don't have any X's, and people in Playland don't have any O's. What is a possible solution to this problem? ***People in the two countries can trade game pieces that they have for game pieces they don't have.***

B. What are the benefits to the citizens of Playland and Gameland if they trade? ***There will be sets available so the citizens of both countries will be able to play Tic-Tac-Toe.***

21. Tell the students that they should trade with the students in the other country to get what they don't have. Explain that for each O that Gameland sends to Playland, Playland must

send an X to Gameland. This is a one-for-one trade.

22. After the students have traded, display Visual 14.4. Ask the following questions and record the students' answers on the visual.

A. How many sets of X's and O's does Gameland have after trade? ***Answers will vary.***

B. How many more sets does Gameland have after specialization and trade than before? ***Answers will vary.***

C. How many more sets of X's and O's does Playland have after trade? ***Answers will vary.***

D. How many more sets of X's and O's does Playland have after specialization and trade than before? ***Answers will vary.***

CLOSURE

23. Review Visuals 14.1, 14.2, 14.3 and 14.4 with the students by asking the following questions:

A. How many X's and O's did the people in each country have before specialization? ***This will be the number produced in each country during the first round of production.***

B. What is specialization? ***People make only a few of the goods and services that they consume.***

C. Do the people in each country have more sets after specialization and trade? ***Yes***

D. What was an advantage of people in each country producing both X's and O's? ***They did not have to depend on other countries.***

E. What was a disadvantage of people in each country producing both X's and O's? ***They could not produce as many sets as citizens wanted.***

F. When people in each country specialized and only produced either X's or O's, what was a disadvantage? ***Neither country could play Tic-Tac-Toe because neither had any sets.***

G. What was an advantage of people in both countries trading? ***Both had more sets than they did before.***

H. What is a disadvantage of each country specializing? ***People in each country will now have to depend on people in the other country for something they want.***

I. What is another name for people depending on other people to get something they want? ***Interdependence***

24. (Optional) As a reward, tell the students that workers will be allowed to compete in a Tic-Tac-Toe tournament in their country. Winners of each round will advance to subsequent rounds until a national winner is determined in each country. The national winner in Playland will then play the national winner in Gameland for the world title. Distribute prizes, if available, to the winners.

(**NOTE:** To shorten the time required to play this many games of Tic-Tac-Toe, if two students play to a draw two or three times in a row, then a tie-breaker can be invoked. You can hold an X or an O behind your back and ask one of the two students to say which you are holding. If the student is correct, he or she wins; if not, the other student wins.)

ASSESSMENT

Distribute a copy of Activity 14.1 to each student. Instruct the students to complete the assessment. Allow time for the students to work. Review answers with the students.

Answers:

1. If everyone in your country produced only X's, how many X's would have been produced? ***A number equal to the number of workers in Gameland, a number equal to twice the number of workers in Playland***

2. If everyone in your country produced only X's, how many O's would have been produced? ***Zero***

3. When everyone in your country produced either X's or O's, how many X's were produced? ***Check answers for both Gameland and Playland from Visual 14.1.***

4. When everyone in your country produced either X's or O's, how many O's were produced? ***Check answers for both Gameland and Playland from Visual 14.1.***

5. If everyone in your country produced only O's, how many X's would have been produced? ***Zero***

6. If everyone in your country produced only O's, how many O's would have been produced? ***A number equal to the number of workers in Playland, a number equal to twice the number of workers in Gameland***

7. List an advantage of people in a country deciding to specialize in what they do best and then trade. ***People will have more products (or more of the products) than without specialization and trade.***

8. List one disadvantage of people in a country deciding to specialize in what they do best and then trade. ***Countries will have to depend on others for products they would like to have.***

Visual 14.1 - **Tic-Tac-Toe Trade**

Each worker in Game-land can produce either

2 O's   or   1 X

Each worker in Playland can produce either

1 O   or   2 X's

Visual 14.2 - **Tic-Tac-Toe Trade**

Production before Trade

Gameland		Playland	
X's	O's	X's	O's
____	____	____	____

Total Number of Sets of X's and O's Produced by Gameland = ________

Total Number of Sets of X's and O's Produced by Playland = ________

Total Number of Sets of X's and O's Produced by Both Countries = ________

Visual 14.3 - **Tic-Tac-Toe Trade**

Production after Specialization

Gameland		Playland	
X's	O's	X's	O's
____	____	____	____

Total Number of Sets of X's and O's Produced by Gameland = __________

Total Number of Sets of X's and O's Produced by Playland = __________

Total Number of Sets of X's and O's Produced by Both Countries = __________

Visual 14.4 - **Tic-Tac-Toe Trade**

Consumption after Trade

Gameland		Playland	
X's	O's	X's	O's
___	___	___	___

How Many Sets of X's and O's Does Gameland Have after Trade? ________

Visual 14.4 - (continued) **Tic-Tac-Toe Trade**

How Many More Sets Does Gameland Have after Specialization and Trade than Before? ____________

How Many Sets of X's and O's Does Playland Have after Trade?

____

How Many More Sets Does Playland Have after Specialization and Trade than Before?

____

Activity 14.1 - **Assessment**

Use your country's results to answer the following questions.

1. If everyone in your country produced only X's, how many X's would have been produced? ____________________

2. If everyone in your country produced only X's, how many O's would have been produced? ____________________

3. When everyone in your country produced either X's or O's, how many X's were produced? ____________________

4. When everyone in your country produced either X's or O's, how many O's were produced? ____________________

5. If everyone in your country produced only O's, how many X's would have been produced? ____________________

6. If everyone in your country produced only O's, how many O's would have been produced? ____________________

7. List one advantage when people in a country decide to specialize in what they do best and then trade. ____________________

   ____

8. List one disadvantage when people in a country decide to specialize in what they do best and then trade. ____________________

   ____

Glossary of Terms

Bank: an institution where people save money and earn interest and where other people borrow money and pay interest (Lesson 9)

Capital resources (goods): goods produced and used to make other goods and services. They are the tools used in the production process. (Lessons 1 and 5)

Characteristics of money: a good medium of exchange has all five of the following characteristics: it is portable, durable, divisible, generally acceptable and relatively scarce (Lesson 10)

Simplified circular flow: a model that shows the interaction of households and businesses in markets in the economy (Lesson 13)

Consumers: people who buy and use goods and services (Lessons 11 and 13)

Entrepreneurs: people who are willing to take risks to develop new products or start businesses. They have an idea for a product, make the product and try to sell the product (Lesson 6)

Goods: things that people use and can touch (Lesson 12)

Government-provided goods and services: goods and services that government provides its citizens and pays for by collecting taxes and fees from individuals and businesses and by borrowing (Lessons 3 and 4)

Human resources: people who work to produce a good or service (Lessons 1, 2, 5 and 7)

Income: the money people receive for the resources they provide in the economy (Lessons 4 and 9)

Income tax: a tax based on the amount of income earned by a person or business in a year (Lesson 4)

Innovation: an invention that has a use to people, and an invention from which inventors can earn profits (Lesson 6)

Interdependence: people must depend on other people to get the things they want (Lesson 14)

Interest: the price people pay for using other people's money (Lesson 9)

Intermediate goods: produced goods used in the production process. They provide the materials with which goods are produced (Lessons 1 and 5)

Law of demand: when the price of a product increases, consumers will buy less of it and when the price of a product decreases, consumers will buy more of it. (Lesson 11)

Loss: occurs when total revenue is less than total cost of production (Lesson 5)

Money: anything widely used as final payment for goods and services (Lesson 10)

Natural resources: things that occur naturally in the world and can be used to produce a good or service. These resources are gifts of nature and are present without human intervention (Lessons 1, 2 and 5)

Opportunity cost: the best alternative given up when a decision is made (Lesson 2)

Opportunity recognition: the first step in solving a problem (Lesson 6)

Price: the amount people pay when they buy a good or service, what they receive when they sell a good or service (Lessons 8 and 11)

Glossary of Terms (continued)

Private goods and services: goods and services produced by private businesses and sold to consumers (Lesson 3)

Producers: people who use resources to make goods and services (Lessons 12 and 13)

Productive resources: the things used to produce a good or service (Lesson 1)

Productivity: the amount of output produced per worker in a given amount of time (Lesson 7)

Profit: the difference between the total revenue a business receives and the total cost it pays for resources. Profit is income for entrepreneurs and is an incentive that encourages them to risk their money and resources. (Lessons 5 and 6)

Property tax: a tax based on the value of a person's or business's property (Lesson 4)

Sales tax: a tax based on the price of purchased goods and services (Lesson 4)

Scarcity: the condition of not being able to have all of the goods and services one wants. It exists because human wants for goods and services exceed the quantity of goods and services that can be produced using all available resources. (Lesson 2)

Services: activities that someone does for us (Lesson 12)

Specialization of labor: occurs when human resources (workers) perform only a single, or very few, step(s) in the production of a product, as they do when working on an assembly line (Lesson 7)

Specialization/Specialization of production: occurs when a group (or individual) produces a smaller range of goods and services than they consume (Lessons 7 and 14)

Taxes: money collected by government from individuals and businesses to pay for goods and services it provides. Taxes are required payments to government. (Lessons 3 and 4)

Total cost: the cost of all of the inputs used to produce a product; the cost of all natural resources, human resources, capital goods and intermediate goods used to produce a product (Lesson 5)

Total revenue: the selling price for a product multiplied by the number of products sold (Lesson 5)

Trade: exchanging goods, services and resources for other goods, services and resources, or for money (Lesson 14)